CRITICAL APPROACHES TO
MARK TWAIN'S SHORT STORIES

Kennikat Press
National University Publications
Literary Criticism Series

CRITICAL APPROACHES TO

MARK TWAIN's

SHORT STORIES

Edited by

ELIZABETH McMAHAN

National University Publications
KENNIKAT PRESS // 1981
Port Washington, N.Y. // London

Manufactured in the United States of America

Published by
Kennikat Press Corp.
Port Washington, N.Y. / London

Library of Congress Cataloging in Publication Data
Main entry under title:

Critical approaches to Mark Twain's short stories.

(National university publications: Literary criticism series)
Bibliography: p. 143
Includes index.
1. Clemens, Samuel Langhorne, 1835–1910–
Criticism and interpretation–Addresses, essays,
lectures. I. McMahan, Elizabeth.
PS1338.C7   813'.4   80-19026
ISBN 0-8046-9274-2

The selections from "the Art of Mark Twain" by
William M. Gibson copyright © 1976 By Oxford
University Press, Inc. are reprinted by permission.

CONTENTS

PREFACE

This collection of criticism on Mark Twain's short stories is designed to be of use to teachers and students. Following an introductory section, the arrangement is chronological: first, in sections according to publication dates of the individual stories; then, within these sections according to the publication date of each essay. All of the stories examined here—with one exception—are included in Charles Neider's widely used text, *The Complete Short Stories of Mark Twain.* Page references have been changed, when necessary, to conform to this inexpensive edition. Many of the stories in Neider's collection make good reading but are not suitable for teaching and have received so little critical attention that no references to them have been included in this volume.

The one story—tale? sketch?—omitted by Neider that deserves teaching is "The Facts Concerning the Recent Carnival of Crime in Connecticut," that fanciful account by a first-person narrator of the murder of his conscience. This piece is readily available in another excellent, but smaller, paperback collection edited by Edmund Reiss, *The Mysterious Stranger and Other Stories.*

Walter Blair reminds us, in his introduction to *Selected Shorter Writings of Mark Twain,* that "for nearly two decades before attempting to compose a full-length book from scratch, Samuel Langhorne Clemens wrote only short pieces." The quality of these numerous short works is, of course, uneven, but without question Twain became one of our finest masters of short fiction in America. Charles Neider considers the short stories often superior to Twain's longer words because "the impulse or the need to pad was at a minimum. . . . One might even say that Twain felt most at home in the story, that it was the form most congenial to him, lover as he was of the yarn" (pp. xiv, xvii-xix). William Gibson agrees that Twain's "talent, his span of attention and concentration perhaps, worked best and most unremittingly in relatively short pieces of writing." As Walter Blair points out, Twain "works best in small compass"; the "works which—as wholes—show Twain coming closest to perfection are all short" (p. viii).

This collection of criticism makes easily accessible the insights of a number of scholars who can help to further our appreciation of Twain's artful short works.

The footnotes which appeared initially in these selections have been eliminated. Readers who are interested in scholarly documentation may consult the original sources, cited on the first page of each essay. Whenever the notes contain crucial information, this material has been included in brackets within the text.

A selected bibliography including items for further study appears at the end of this collection.

CRITICAL APPROACHES TO MARK TWAIN'S SHORT STORIES

ABOUT THE EDITOR

Elizabeth McMahan is a professor of English at Illinois State University in Normal, Illinois. She has received awards for her critical writing. She is the author of articles on Mark Twain in the *Mark Twain Journal,* and the *Illinois Quarterly,* as well as articles on Henry James, John Steinbeck, Ken Kesey, and on the teaching of poetry. She is also author or coauthor of several books and articles on composition and language.

1

HOW MARK TWAIN WRITES

Mark Twain frequently—and often insightfully—explained how writing should be done. George Feinstein's essay, the last in this introductory section, provides a valuable summary of Twain's major literary principles. The first selection, written by Twain in 1870, is a little-known piece salvaged by M. B. Fried from the files of the Buffalo *Express,* in which Twain justifies the choice of two prize-winning essays from a contest he helped judge while editor of the Buffalo paper. Although his observations pertain to these narrative essays, he reveals in his comments several characteristics that he values in short stories. As Charles Neider rightly observes, "Twain was a man who was very easy-going about border lines" (pp. xi-xii).

In the middle selection, "How to Tell a Story" (1894), Twain presents his views concerning oral interpretation. Since Twain's is essentially an oral style, these remarks are germane to his written works as well. William Gibson points out that he used punctuation to convey in writing the "high and delicate art" of the pause (p. 20). Twain also analyzes in the course of this essay one of his most effective writing techniques, the "innocently unaware" narrative persona—a device employed to perfection in the portrayal of the garrulous Simon Wheeler, who meanders his way through the celebrated story of the jumping frog.

S. L. CLEMENS
REPORT TO THE BUFFALO FEMALE ACADEMY

I beg leave to offer the report of the committee appointed to sit in judgment upon the compositions of the graduating and collegiate classes. We have done our work carefully and conscientiously; we have determined the degrees of literary excellence displayed, with pitiless honesty; we have experienced no sort of difficulty in selecting and agreeing upon the two first-prize compositions—and yet, after all, we feel that it is necessary to say a word or two in vindication of our verdict.

Because, we have misgivings that our choice might not be the choice of the Academy, if the choice were left to them—nor of this assembly—nor a vote of the general public. Let this comfort those fair competitors whom our verdict has wronged. But we have judged these compositions by the strict rules of literary criticism, and let this reassure those whom our verdict has exalted.

We have chosen as the two prize essays the least showy of the eighteen submitted, perhaps, but they are the least artificial, the least labored, the clearest and shapeliest, and the best carried out. The paper we have chosen for the first prize of the graduates is very much the best literary effort in the whole collection, and yet it is almost the least ambitious among them. It relates a very simple little incident, in unpretentious language, and then achieves the difficult feat of pointing it with one of those dismal atrocities called a Moral, without devoting double the space to it which it ought to occupy and outraging every canon of good taste, relevancy and modesty. It is a composition which possesses, also, the very rare merit of *stopping when it is finished.* It shows a freedom from adjectives and superlatives which is attractive, not to say seductive—and let us remark instructively, in passing, that one can seldom run his pen through an adjective without improving his manuscript. We can say further, in praise of this first-class composition, that there is a singular aptness of language noticeable in it—denoting a shrewd faculty of selecting just the right word for the service needed, as a general thing. It is a high gift. It is the talent which gives accuracy, grace and vividness in descriptive writing.

The other first prize—the collegiate—is so simple and unpretending that it seems a daring thing to prefer it before certain of its fellows which we could name, but still we of the committee rigidly decree that it is perceptibly superior to the best of them. It is nothing in the world but

---

From *Mark Twain on the Art of Writing,* ed. M. B. Fried (Buffalo, N. Y.: The Salisbury Club, 1961), pp. 1-10.

just a bright and fresh bit of fancy, told with a breezy dash, and with nothing grand or overpowering about it. Attached to it is the inevitable Moral, but it is compressed into a single sentence, and it is delivered with a snap that is exhilarating and an unexpectedness that is captivating. And we are furthermore able to say, in justification of the Moral, that the composition would not be symmetrical, keenly and clearly pointed and complete, without it. An application, or a "nub," or a moral that *fits,* is a jewel of price. It is only the awkward, irrelevant and pinchbeck moral that this committee snubs.

Now, if you have observed, we have decided that the graduates' first prize possesses the several merits of unpretentiousness, simplicity of language and subject, and marked aptness and accuracy of wording—and that the collegiate first-prize has the merits of modesty and freshness of subject and grace and excellence of treatment. But both of these possess one other merit, or cluster of merits, which strongly attracted us. They were *instinct* with naturalness—a most noble and excellent feature in composition, and one which is customarily lacking in productions written for state occasions, from the Friday compositions in a village school all the way up to the President's message—and you may verify my words by critically examining any written speech that ever *was* written—except this one that I am reading. The two prize essays possess naturalness, and likewise a happy freshness that marks them as the expression of the original thoughts and fancies of the minds that wrought them, and not stale and venerable platitudes and commonplaces absorbed from good but stupid books and drowsy sermons and delivered at second hand in the same unvarying and monotonous sequence—a sequence which they have grown so familiar with since Adam and each of his descendants in turn used them in his appointed season, that now one needs only write down the first of them and the rest fall into line without a murmur or ever a missing veteran.

We consider it a plain duty to observe that while the disposition in all school compositions to contemplate all subjects from high moral and religious altitudes would be a matter for sincere praise and gratulation, if such disposition came from a strong spontaneous impulse on the part of the student, it is not matter for praise or gratulation either when that disposition is strained or forced. Nearly all the compositions submitted to us would have been right creditable specimens of literary handiwork, if the sermons had been left out of them. But, while some of these latter were the expression of a genuine impulse, the great majority of them were so manifestly dragged in and hitched on to the essay (out of pure force of habit and therefore unconsciously, we are willing to believe, but still plainly dragged in), that they sadly marred some of the compositions and entirely spoiled one or two. Religion is the highest and holiest thing on earth, and a strained or compulsory expression of it is not gracious, or commendable, or befitting its dignity.

However, we have the hardihood to say, in this place, that considering the "Standard School Readers" and other popular and unspeakably execrable models which young people are defrauded into accepting as fine literary composition, the real wonder is, not that pupils attempt subjects which they would be afraid of at forty, and then write floridly instead of simply, and start without premises and wind up without tangible result, but that they write at all without bringing upon themselves suspicions of imbecility.

The dead weight of custom and tradition have clogged school method and discipline from a past date which we cannot name, until the present time. . . . When the old sapless composition model is finally cast entirely aside and the pupil learns to write straight from his heart, he will apply his own language and his own ideas to his subjects and then the question with committees will not be which composition to select for first prize, but which one they dare reject.

S. L. CLEMENS
HOW TO TELL A STORY

I do not claim that I can tell a story as it ought to be told. I only claim to know how a story ought to be told, for I have been almost daily in the company of the most expert story-tellers for many years.

There are several kinds of stories, but only one difficult kind—the humorous. I will talk mainly about that one. The humorous story is American, the comic story is English, the witty story is French. The humorous story depends for its effect upon the *manner* of the telling; the comic story and the witty story about the *matter.*

The humorous story may be spun out to great length, and may wander around as much as it pleases, and arrive nowhere in particular, but the comic and witty stories must be brief and end with a point. The humorous story bubbles gently along, the others burst.

The humorous story is strictly a work of art—high and delicate art—

From *How to Tell a Story and Other Essays* (New York: Harper & Brothers, 1900), pp. 7-12. Reprinted by permission of Harper & Row, Publishers, Inc.

and only an artist can tell it; but no art is necessary in telling the comic and the witty story; anybody can do it. The art of telling a humorous story—understand, I mean by word of mouth, not print—was created in America, and has remained at home.

The humorous story is told gravely; the teller does his best to conceal the fact that he even dimly suspects that there is anything funny about it; but the teller of the comic story tells you beforehand that it is one of the funniest things he has ever heard, then tells it with eager delight, and is the first person to laugh when he gets through. And sometimes, if he has had good success, he is so glad and happy that he will repeat the "nub" of it and glance around from face to face, collecting applause, and then repeat it again. It is a pathetic thing to see.

Very often, of course, the rambling and disjointed humorous story finishes with a nub, point, snapper, or whatever you like to call it. Then the listener must be alert, for in many cases the teller will divert attention from that nub by dropping it in a carefully casual and indifferent way, with the pretence that he does not know it is a nub.

Artemus Ward used that trick a good deal; then when the belated audience presently caught the joke he would look up with innocent surprise, as if wondering what they had found to laugh at. Dan Setchell used it before him, Nye and Riley and others use it to-day.

But the teller of the comic story does not slur the nub; he shouts it at you—every time. And when he prints it, in England, France, Germany, and Italy, he italicizes it, puts some whooping exclamation-points after it, and sometimes explains it in a parenthesis. All of which is very depressing, and makes one want to renounce joking and lead a better life.

Let me set down an instance of the comic method, using an anecdote which has been popular all over the world for twelve or fifteen hundred years. The teller tells it in this way:

The Wounded Soldier.

In the course of a certain battle a soldier whose leg had been shot off appealed to another soldier who was hurrying by to carry him to the rear, informing him at the same time of the loss which he had sustained; whereupon the generous son of Mars, shouldering the unfortunate, proceeded to carry out his desire. The bullets and cannon-balls were flying in all directions, and presently one of the latter took the wounded man's head off—without, however, his deliverer being aware of it. In no long time he was hailed by an officer who said:

"Where are you going with that carcass?"

"To the rear, sir—he's lost his leg!"

"His leg, forsooth?" responded the astonished officer; "you mean his head, you booby."

Whereupon the soldier dispossessed himself of his burden, and stood looking down upon it in great perplexity. At length he said:

"It is true, sur, just as you have said." Then after a pause he added, "But he *told* me *it was his leg*!!!!"

Here the narrator bursts into explosion after explosion of thunderous horse-laughter, repeating that nub from time to time through his gaspings and shriekings and suffocatings.

It takes only a minute and half to tell that in its comic-story form; and isn't worth the telling, after all. Put into the humorous-story form it takes ten minutes, and is about the funniest thing I have ever listened to— as James Whitcomb Riley tells it.

He tells it in the character of a dull-witted old farmer who has just heard it for the first time, thinks it unspeakably funny, and is trying to repeat it to a neighbor. But he can't remember it; so he gets all mixed up and wanders helplessly round and round, putting in tedious details that don't belong in the tale and only retard it; taking them out conscientiously and putting in others that are just as useless; making minor mistakes now and then and stopping to correct them and explain how he came to make them; remembering things which he forgot to put in in their proper place and going back to put them in there; stopping his narrative a good while in order to try to recall the name of the soldier that was hurt, and finally remembering that the soldier's name was not mentioned, and remarking placidly that the name is of no real importance, anyway—better, of course, if one knew it, but not essential after all—and so on, and so on, and so on.

The teller is innocent and happy and pleased with himself, and has to stop every little while to hold himself in and keep from laughing outright; and does hold in, but his body quakes in a jelly-like way with interior chuckles; and at the end of the ten minutes the audience have laughed until they are exhausted, and the tears are running down their faces.

The simplicity and innocence and sincerity and unconsciousness of the old farmer are perfectly simulated, and the result is a performance which is thoroughly charming and delicious. This is art—and fine and beautiful, and only a master can compass it; but a machine could tell the other story.

To string incongruities and absurdities together in a wandering and sometimes purposeless way, and seem innocently unaware that they are absurdities, is the basis of the American art, if my position is correct. Another feature is the slurring of the point. A third is the dropping of a studied remark apparently without knowing it, as if one were thinking aloud. The fourth and last is the pause.

Artemus Ward dealt in numbers three and four a good deal. He would begin to tell with great animation something which he seemed to think was wonderful; then lose confidence, and after an apparently absent-minded pause add an incongruous remark in a soliloquizing way; and that was the remark intended to explode the mine—and it did.

For instance, he would say eagerly, excitedly, "I once knew a man in New Zealand who hadn't a tooth in his head"—here his animation would die out; a silent, reflective pause would follow, then he would say dreamily, and as if to himself, "and yet that man could beat a drum better than any man I ever saw."

The pause is an exceedingly important feature in any kind of story, and a frequently recurring feature, too. It is a dainty thing, and delicate, and also uncertain and treacherous; for it must be exactly the right length—no more and no less—or it fails of its purpose and makes trouble. If the pause is too short the impressive point is passed, and the audience have had time to divine that a surprise is intended—and then you can't surprise them, of course.

* * * * * * *

GEORGE FEINSTEIN
MARK TWAIN'S IDEA OF STORY STRUCTURE

Clemens's conception of story form departs sharply from the views sanctified by critical tradition. He opposes a studied perfection of plot, favors instead a loose, spontaneous development of narrative: ". . . narrative should flow as flows the brook down through the hills and the leafy woodlands, its course changed by every bowlder." The customary narrative stream he likens to a canal: ". . . it moves slowly, smoothly, decorously, sleepily, it has no blemish except that it is all blemish. It is too literary, too prim, too nice; the gait and style and movement are not suited to narrative." The basic notion is venerable: *Ars est artem celare* [Artistry conceals its art] . But the novelty is that Mark Twain, with a humorist's sensitivity, is unprecedently alive to what he considers to be formal, therefore planned and undesirable, effects in story construction. Ideal narration, he insists, is natural and informal, like life or talk.

From *American Literature,* 18 (1946), pp. 160-163. Copyright 1946 by Duke University Press. Reprinted by permission of Duke University Press.

A tale then must grow organically, from within, or the artificiality will show. It must "tell itself," the author simply holding the pen. Lacking such spontaneous origin it becomes "a piece of pure literary manufacture and has the shopmarks all over it." His own method, he tells us, is to take some characters, one or two incidents, and a locality, plunge them together hopefully, and listen to the story as it goes along, spreading itself into a book. To compose like this requires a gift, he admits; but the ungifted should not write novels.

The sacredness of story structure, which Twain has in effect challenged, is rooted in Aristotelian theory. It appears in the modern period in the short story tradition of Irving-Poe-Hawthorne. A main action, with beginning, middle, and end, a dominating character, a complication, a climax —these historic essentials get scant homage in Clemens's criticism and practice. "The world," he says, "grows tired of solid forms in all the arts." Poe's theory of unity of effect—every atom of plot to be streamlined and irreplaceable—is largely ignored. Manifestly, Twain's anomalous stricture on the disconnected episodes in the *Deerslayer* proceeds rather from his failure to feel any real inner psychological movement linking that novel's episodes than from any actual aesthetic impulse toward external unity.

Compression, tonal unity, the three unities of French classic drama— none of these are inviolable. Clemens's one consideration is that a story, an experience, be given the reader; "the how of it is not important." "The Jumping Frog," "Adam's Diary," "Eve's Diary," and the "McWilliams" stories present not plots but rather situations. These stories are rambling and amorphous, vitalized chiefly by their mass of human quirks and small incident—they illustrate their author's conviction that execution transcends design. Again, his indifference to arbitrary canons governing story structure is marked in "Captain Stormfield's Visit to Heaven" and "The Stolen White Elephant"; it is egregious in the final chapters of *Huckleberry Finn.*

Mark Twain values, not the architectonic effect of a tale, but the art of the paragraph, the sentence, the illuminating incident. Journalism has furnished him the training. As critic he knows well, and demands, the spicy fare—humor, pathos, variety—which holds a newsreader's eye. His own humor, born of journalism, is in essence paragraphic, episodic, inconsequential; like the humor of Cervantes, Rabelais, and Sterne it shuns symmetrical pattern as a violation of its nature. The spirit of this humor has helped to shape his notion of structure. Characteristically, as coeditor of the *Library of Humor* anthology he shuffles [William Dean] Howells's sequential arrangement to suit his own whim.

Form for Clemens is ideally the externalization of an author's thinking. Thinking is personal, informal, digressive; so for him these traits inform honest writing in all genres. In autobiography, he particularly recommends discursiveness, the free play of fancy. A thing recollected should be jammed in as it occurs to the memoirist, not put into an earlier chapter. He anticipates stream-of-consciousness portraiture, notably in the garrulousness of characters like Jim Blaine in *Roughing It,* but specifically in his theory of autobiography. In ideal autobiography, things of the present are to be juxtaposed with "memories of like things in the past." *"The thing uppermost in a person's mind* is the thing to talk about or write about."* He holds that "sleeping or waking, dreaming or talking, the thoughts which swarm through our heads are almost constantly, almost continuously, accompanied by a like swarm of reminders of incidents and episodes of our past." To our inner consciousness big incidents and little incidents have the same size. A man's life really consists mainly of his feelings and interests, he asserts; thus the autobiographer's herculean job is to reflect "the storm of thoughts that is forever blowing through one's head."

Since literary work is so closely attuned to the author's mental processes, its form clearly becomes an individual matter. The difficulty, as Clemens sees it, is to get properly started—that is, to ascertain the sole form so natural to the writer's mentality that the work will slide effortlessly from his pen. Literary form is plainly for him a function of personality rather than of genre. Significantly, his own best essays and short stories, products of the nineties, are animated by an identical, and idiosyncratic, spirit and method—a method apparently of methodlessness; and the form of *Life on the Mississippi* belongs not to history, or travels, or novel—simply to Mark Twain.

2

THE CELEBRATED JUMPING FROG
OF CALAVERAS COUNTY

With the coming of the Civil War and the closing of the Mississippi River, Twain was forced to abandon his prestigious position as steamboat pilot. He briefly became a lieutenant in the Confederate army, but his sympathies concerning the war were divided and military life was not to his liking. When his brother Orion was appointed Territorial Secretary of Nevada, Twain, as Kenneth S. Lynn puts it, "leaped at the chance to secede from Sucession and go along as secretary to the Secretary." While out West, he engaged in both newspaper writing and mining, vocations which happily coincided to produce "The Celebrated Jumping Frog."

As Albert Bigelow Paine, Twain's "official" biographer, relates in the first piece in this section, the "Jumping Frog" story was suggested by a tale Twain heard in the mining camps. Other articles in the section make clear that the story is actually much older in origin, having roots in Negro folklore and Athenian fable. Significantly, Twain was the first person to record the story with artistry.

When first published as "Jim Smiley and His Jumping Frog" in the New York *Saturday Press* (November 18, 1865), the work won instant acclaim. The San Francisco *Alta* reported, "Mark Twain's story . . . has set all New York in a roar, and he may have been said to have made his mark . . . . It is voted the best thing of the day." Twain himself describes its publication with modesty and humor. In the "Private History of the 'Jumping Frog,'" he says that when publisher Henry Clapp put the story in his *Saturday Press,*

. . . it killed that paper with a suddenness that was beyond praise. At least the paper died with that issue, and none but envious people have ever tried to rob me of the honor and credit of killing it. The "Jumping

Frog" was the first piece of writing of mine that spread itself through the newspapers and brought me into public notice. Consequently, the *Saturday Press* was a cocoon and I the worm within it; also, I was the gay-colored literary moth which its death set free.

Readers and critics alike, as the following essays attest, continue to judge the "Jumping Frog" one of Twain's finest short stories.

ALBERT BIGELOW PAINE
THE JUMPING FROG

It was the rainy season, the winter of 1864 and 1865, but there were many pleasant days, when they could go pocket-hunting, and Samuel Clemens soon added a knowledge of this fascinating science to his other acquirements. Sometimes he worked with Dick Stoker, sometimes with one of the Gillis boys. He did not make his fortune at pocket-mining; he only laid its corner-stone. In the old note-book he kept of that sojourn we find that, with Jim Gillis, he made a trip over into Calaveras County soon after Christmas and remained there until after New Year's, probably prospecting; and he records that on New Year's night, at Vallecito, he saw a magnificent lunar rainbow in a very light, drizzling rain. A lunar rainbow is one of the things people seldom see. He thought it an omen of good-fortune.

They returned to the cabin on the hill; but later in the month, on the 23d, they crossed over into Calaveras again, and began pocket-hunting not far from Angel's Camp. The note-book records that the bill of fare at the Camp hotel consisted wholly of beans and something which bore the name of coffee; also that the rains were frequent and heavy.

January 27. Same old diet—same old weather—went out to the pocket-claim—had to rush back.

They had what they believed to be a good claim. Jim Gillis declared the indications promising, and if they could only have good weather to work it, they were sure of rich returns. For himself, he would have been willing to

---

From *Mark Twain: A Biography* (3 vols., New York: Harper and Brothers, 1912), 1, pp. 270–273. Reprinted by permission of Harper & Row, Publishers, Inc.

work, rain or shine. Clemens, however, had different views on the subject. His part was carrying water for washing out the pans of dirt, and carrying pails of water through the cold rain and mud was not very fascinating work. Dick Stoker came over before long to help. Things went a little better then; but most of their days were spent in the bar-room of the dilapidated tavern at Angel's Camp, enjoying the company of a former Illinois River pilot, Ben Coon, a solemn, fat-witted person, who dozed by the stove, or told slow, endless stories, without point or application. Listeners were a boon to him, for few came and not many would stay. To Mark Twain and Jim Gillis, however, Ben Coon was a delight. It was soothing and comfortable to listen to his endless narratives, told in that solemn way, with no suspicion of humor. Even when his yarns had point, he did not recognize it. One dreary afternoon, in his slow, monotonous fashion, he told them about a frog—a frog that had belonged to a man named Coleman, who trained it to jump, but that failed to win a wager because the owner of a rival frog had surreptitiously loaded the trained jumper with shot. The story had circulated among the camps, and a well-known journalist, named Samuel Seabough, had already made a squib of it, but neither Clemens nor Gillis had ever happened to hear it before. They thought the tale in itself amusing, and the "spectacle of a man drifting serenely along through such a queer yarn without ever smiling was exquisitely absurd." When Coon had talked himself out, his hearers played billiards on the frowsy table, and now and then one would remark to the other:

"I don't see no p'ints about that frog that's any better'n any other frog," and perhaps the other would answer:

"I ain't got no frog, but if I had a frog I'd bet you."

Out on the claim, between pails of water, Clemens, as he watched Jim Gillis or Dick Stoker "washing," would be apt to say, "I don't see no p'ints about that pan o' dirt that's any better'n any other pan o' dirt," and so they kept it up.

Then the rain would come again and interfere with their work. One afternoon, when Clemens and Gillis were following certain tiny-sprayed specks of gold that were leading them to a pocket somewhere up the long slope, the chill downpour set in. Gillis, as usual, was washing, and Clemens carrying water. The "color" was getting better with every pan, and Jim Gillis believed that now, after their long waiting, they were to be rewarded. Possessed with the miner's passion, he would have gone on washing and climbing toward the precious pocket, regardless of everything. Clemens, however, shivering and disgusted, swore that each pail of water was his last. His teeth were chattering and he was wet through. Finally he said, in his deliberate way:

"Jim I won't carry any more water. This work is too disagreeable."

Gillis had just taken out a panful of dirt.

"Bring one more pail, Sam," he pleaded.

"Oh, hell, Jim, I won't do it; I'm freezing!"

"Just one more pail, Sam," he pleaded.

"No, sir, not a drop, not if I knew there were a million dollars in that pan."

Gillis tore a page out of his note-book, and hastily posted a thirty-day claim notice by the pan of dirt, and they set out for Angel's Camp. It kept on raining and storming, and they did not go back. A few days later a letter from Steve Gillis made Clemens decide to return to San Francisco. With Jim Gillis and Dick Stoker he left Angel's and walked across the mountains to Jackass Hill in the snow-storm—"the first I ever saw in California," he says in his notes.

In the mean time the rain had washed away the top of the pan of earth they had left standing on the hillside, and exposed a handful of nuggets—pure gold. Two strangers, Austrians, had come along and, observing it, had sat down to wait until the thirty-day claim notice posted by Jim Gillis should expire. They did not mind the rain—not with all that gold in sight—and the minute the thirty days were up they followed the lead a few pans farther and took out—some say ten, some say twenty, thousand dollars. In either case it was a good pocket. Mark Twain missed it by one pail of water. Still, it is just as well, perhaps, when one remembers that vaster nugget of Angel's Camp—the Jumping Frog. Jim Gillis always declared, "If Sam had got that pocket he would have remained a pocket-miner to the end of his days, like me."

In Mark Twain's old note-book occurs a memorandum of the frog story—a mere casual entry of its main features:

Coleman with his jumping frog—bet stranger $50—stranger had no frog, and C. got him one:—in the mean time stranger filled C.'s frog full of shot and he couldn't jump. The stranger's frog won.

It seemed unimportant enough, no doubt, at the time; but it was the nucleus around which was built a surpassing fame. The hills along the Stanislaus have turned out some wonderful nuggets in their time, but no other of such size as that.

GLADYS BELLAMY
THE ART OF "THE JUMPING FROG"

In Mark Twain's frontier years there is no taint of the self-consciousness, the patronizing tone, which blemishes the native portaiture of Bret Harte. Instead, Mark Twain's work is distinguished by its complete naturalness, a quality belonging to the art which seems no art; but art of that sort is rarely attained except by painstaking care. Among these native materials, he appears to have worked with utter freedom. Harte, Easterner as he was, seems to have been gripped by the theatrical aspects of the California scene. Mark Twain, too, appreciated the drama of that life, but he did not seek for scenes heightened in dramatic intensity. He realized that, strange and odd as some of these creatures might appear before the painted backdrop of mountain and sea, down underneath they were actually people. The same sort of naturalness covers his oddest characters.

His early frontier figures are presented with a primitive spontaneity. He makes no effort at the realization of an extended character, as yet. Still, in his early isolated portraits he exhibits a serenity that offers a striking contrast to the impatience with mankind that pricks him on in his satiric or moralistic sketches. We find here no cynical sport arrayed in the verbal pyrotechnics of the humorist virtuoso. [As Santayana observes in "The Nature of Beauty,"] "The struggle has ended, the pain has died away," and the writer dominates and controls his material to the point where serenity at last becomes possible. He neither admires nor abhors the creatures of these frontier sketches; he simply understands them. And his complete understanding of their behavior and thought gives him an enjoyment reflected in his work—leads him finally into the true aesthetic attitude, which challenges the writer to present his material artistically, taking his joy in the authenticity of his product without concern for the didactic element. With his facility in copying speech rhythms, vocal intonations, native idioms and mannerisms, he was rapidly approaching artistic performance in native portraiture. It was in this field that he would become an artist.

Almost from the first he touched up his frontier portraits with an imaginative brush. Ben Coon appears in his own person to tell the story of his dictionary; but by the time of "The Jumping Frog" he has become, for literary purposes, "good-natured, garrulous old Simon Wheeler." In

From *Mark Twain as a Literary Artist*, pp. 146-149. Copyright 1950 by the University of Oklahoma Press, publishing division of the University. Reprinted by permission (title is editor's).

the earlier sketch Mark Twain gave but a passing glance to the "shade of melancholy" which flitted across Coon's face before he began his recital; but in the Frog, one of the most effective bits is the powerful spotlight which is turned on the narrator and his method:

He never smiled, he never frowned, he never changed his voice from the gentle-flowing key to which he turned his initial sentence, he never betrayed the slightest suspicion of enthusiasm; but all through the interminable narrative there ran a vein of impressive earnestness and sincerity, which showed me plainly that, so far from his imagining that there was anything ridiculous or funny about his story, he regarded it as a really important matter, and admired its two heroes as men of transcendent genius in *finesse*. I let him go on in his own way and never interrupted him once.

As Walter Blair has observed, a part of the excellence of "The Jumping Frog" arises from Mark Twain's skillful management of the narrative framework. This frame holds three successive personalities: first there is Mark Twain, writing in his own person to Artemus Ward; Mark Twain then presents Simon Wheeler; Wheeler, in his turn, presents Jim Smiley and the stranger. And, as Miss Brashear points out, the tale gets its peculiar quality from being the report of one oddity by another; for Jim Smiley is as intensely interesting to Simon Wheeler as Wheeler himself is interesting to Mark Twain. Within the Wheeler yarn, there is a careful climactic arrangement: first we have that talented mare, the "fifteen-minute nag"; then the "little small bull-pup" that would have "made a name for hisself if he'd lived, for the stuff was in him, and he had genius"; and finally the educated frog, Dan'l Webster: "You never see a frog so modest and straight-for'ard as he was, for all he was so gifted." Yet these distinct personalities fade into the background when the clash begins between the two men, with its surprising climax. No moral is pointed, no lesson taught. What followed is literary history. Arriving in New York too late for inclusion in Artemus Ward's new book, the sketch was printed instead in the last issue of the expiring *Saturday Press,* November 18, 1865. From the *Press* it was speedily copied in papers all over the country.

By the time Mark Twain wrote the Ben Coon and Simon Wheeler anecdotes in 1865, he had arrived at most of the knowledge which he incorporated in 1894 into "How to Tell a Story." There he says that the humorous story—the most difficult kind—is American, the comic story is English, and the witty story is French:

The humorous story depends for its effect upon the *manner* of the telling; the comic story and the witty story upon the *matter*. . . . The humorous story bubbles gently along, the others burst.

The humorous story is strictly a work of art—high and delicate art—and only an artist can tell it; but no art is necessary in telling the comic and witty story; anybody can do it. The art of telling a humorous story ... was created in America, and has remained at home.

The humorous story is told gravely; the teller ... conceal[s] the fact that he even dimly suspects that there is anything funny about it; but the teller of the comic story ... is the first person to laugh when he gets through. . . . To string incongruities and absurdities together in a wandering and sometimes purposeless way, and seem innocently unaware that they are absurdities is the basis of the American art.

Mark Twain then comments on the skill with which James Whitcomb Riley told a story in the guise of a dull-witted old farmer whose rambling technique followed the humorous method. He adds: "This is art—and fine and beautiful, and only a master can compass it; but a machine could tell the other story."

KENNETH S. LYNN

UPSET EXPECTATIONS IN "THE JUMPING FROG"

Twain's most interesting literary experiment was "The Celebrated Jumping Frog of Calaveras County," written the year after the author left Nevada. Possibly a Negro tale to begin with—the slyness with which the defeat of the champion is managed would seem to be the distinguishing mark of the slave upon it—the frog story was taken over by the rough-and-tumble society of the mining camps and incorporated in its democratic myth. Various versions of the story had been published in Western newspapers before Mark Twain ever reached California. In appropriating the story for his own purposes, he made numerous changes. First and foremost, he embellished the anecdote with a "frame," in which we are introduced to the narrator, "Mark Twain," who in turn tells us of his encounter with Simon Wheeler in the barroom at Angel's Camp. The narrator's casual reference to an Eastern friend, and his indulgently superior description of the "winning gentleness and simplicity" of Simon Wheeler's countenance, establish his affinity with the Self-controlled Gentleman of the Southwestern tradition, albeit the style of the prose in the "frame" is

From *Mark Twain and the Southwestern Humorists* (Boston: Little, Brown, 1960), pp. 145–47. Reprinted by the permission of the author (title is editor's).

more informal than that of the Longstreet model. The similarities of structure and dramatic situation, however, are sufficient to make us expect the familiar puppet show. The story upsets all our calculations—and the narrator's as well. "Mark Twain," as things turn out, is not as clever as he thinks he is. Assuming himself to be more sophisticated than the man he meets, the encounter teaches him just the reverse—it is he, not Simon, who is simple. The innocence of Simon Wheeler's expression is in fact a mask, cunningly assumed to deceive the outsider by seeming to fulfill all his pre-conceived notions of Western simple-mindedness. Simon Wheeler's little joke, of course, is simply a California variation on the ancient con game of the trans-Allegheny frontiersman, but in literary terms the "Jumping Frog" marks a historic reversal. The narrator, it turns out, is telling a joke on himself, not on the Clown. In the "Jumping Frog," it is the vernacular, not the polite style, which "teaches the lesson." The Southwestern tradition, in other words, has been stood on its head.

The "frame" is a drama of upset expectations, and so is the story proper. Simon launches his vernacular monologue about Jim Smiley (after having been asked for information concerning the Reverend Leonidas W. Smiley) with an ancedote about Jim Smiley's bulldog, who could whip any other dog by fastening his teeth on his opponent's hind leg and hanging on "till they threw up the sponge, if it was a year," but who was finally defeated by a dog "that didn't have no hind legs, because they'd been sawed off in a circular saw. . . ." Doubtless Twain's Whig upbringing had something to do with the fact that the name of Smiley's bulldog is Andrew Jackson, for in making a dog of that name look ridiculous Twain in effect ridiculed a politician who he never ceased to believe had been a disastrous President. Simon Wheeler's ironic praise of the dog—"a good pup, was that Andrew Jackson, and would have made a name for hisself if he'd lived, for the stuff was in him and he had genius—I know it, because he hadn't no opportunities to speak of, and it don't stand to reason that a dog could make such a fight as he could under them circumstances if he hadn't no talent"—would certainly have appealed to the Whiggish sense of humor of the earlier Southwestern writers. When we learn, however, as we do very shortly, that Jim Smiley's frog is named Daniel Webster, in honor of Whiggery's arch-hero, we begin to realize that this story is not playing political favorites in the old way at all, but is in fact saying a plague on both houses of a tragic era. Simon Wheeler's tall tale does not take sides on past history, it rejects the past altogether, and turns toward the West and the future. It also endorses democracy by making fun of superior feelings, as the "frame" had done. Gazing at Daniel Webster, the stranger says, in one of the most famous remarks in the history of American humor, "I don't see no p'ints about that frog that's any better'n any other frog." The subsequent triumph of the anonymous underfrog over the vaunted Daniel Webster comically vindicates the stranger's radical democracy. As the author of the "Jumping Frog" had lately discovered, it didn't pay to be too proud in the West.

Catching the upturn of the national mood at the close of the Civil War, the "Jumping Frog" was an instantaneous success, James Russell Lowell hailing it as "the finest piece of humorous literature yet produced in America." If the story had any flaws, they resided in the character of the narrator. It was not quite certain who "Mark Twain" was. He seemed a more colloquial figure than the Self-controlled Gentleman, yet he continued to play the Gentleman's role, vis-à-vis the Clown. In the period following the publication of the "Jumping Frog," Twain's major imaginative effort was devoted to solving the problem of his narrative persona.

HENRY NASH SMITH

THE MYSTERIOUS CHARM OF SIMON WHEELER

The effect of "Jim Smiley and His Jumping Frog" (1865), the sketch that won for Mark Twain his first national reputation, also depends upon the rather mysterious charm of the vernacular spokesman, Simon Wheeler. Wheeler is a good-natured derelict "dozing comfortably by the bar-room stove of the dilapidated tavern" in the Mother Lode ghost town of Angel's Camp. He is "fat and bald-headed," with "an expression of winning gentleness and simplicity upon his tranquil countenance." Wheeler's simplicity is evident in the fact that he is dazzled by heroic memories of the "transcendent genius" of both Jim Smiley, owner of the celebrated jumping frog, and the stranger who won the bet by filling Smiley's frog with shot. But this simplicity and even the preposterous story about the frog, which was current in the mining camps, are less significant than Wheeler's gentleness and tranquility. He [exhibits] the vernacular traits of basic good will and freedom from the kind of inner conflict suffered by the speaker in "Sabbath Reflections." Left behind in this backwater by the vanished mining boom, he dwells on the elegiac theme of mute

From *Mark Twain: The Development of a Writer* (Cambridge, Mass.: Belknap Press of Harvard University Press), p. 11. Copyright © 1962 by the President and Fellows of Harvard College. Reprinted by permission (title is editor's).

inglorious Miltons. Smiley's handicapped dog Andrew Jackson, he says, "would have made a name for hisself if he'd lived, for the stuff was in him, and he had genius—I know it, because he hadn't no opportunities to speak of, and it don't stand to reason that a dog could make such a fight as he could under them circumstances, if he hadn't no talent." Even Daniel Webster, the frog, is an example of great abilities frustrated by circumstance. "Smiley said all a frog wanted was education, and he could do 'most anything—and I believe him." After three months of intensive training Daniel could "nail a fly every time as fur as he could see him." But he was cheated of the triumph he deserved by the stranger's trick.

Wheeler is however not aware of the note of apology in his tale, and the theme is subordinate to the creation of a grotesque fictive world lacking the stresses imposed on men in the real world who must exhibit approved attitudes in order to achieve power and status. . . . Wheeler is indifferent to the competitive self-consciousness of an acquisitive society. Both characters represent gestures of escape from the pale negations and paler affirmations of the genteel tradition; they are the beginnings of an effort to "express something worth expressing behind its back."

SYDNEY J. KRAUSE
THE ART AND SATIRE OF TWAIN'S "JUMPING FROG" STORY

Recent analyses of Mark Twain's "Notorious Jumping Frog of Calaveras County" tend to stress its projection of the traditional conflict between eastern and western values—or, more precisely, between the values of a gentle, civilized class and those of the frontier. Taking in its broadest potential reference, Paul Schmidt has seen the "Jumping Frog" as dramatizing those assumptions which, as he has it, "make up the complicated Enlightenment case of Civilization versus the West." Moreover, construing the tale as "an attack on the genteel tradition," Schmidt holds that it "ultimately asserts the superiority of vernacular brotherhood over the competitive individualism which animates genteel attitudes"; while in Wheeler's story, the tale within the tale, he sees an attack on Rousseauesque romanticism.

From *American Quarterly*, 16 (Winter 1964), 562-576. Published by the University of Pennsylvania. Copyright 1964, Trustees of the University of Pennsylvania. Reprinted by permission.

Schmidt's analysis seems to involve some high-powered assumptions for a fairly unsophisticated brand of fiction. Yet at least two reasons why the "Jumping Frog" rises above its genre are that its simplicity—like Simon Wheeler's—is ironic and its social symbolism—like Wheeler's story—implies more than it asserts. A major artistic consideration is, therefore, the matter of how the inward moving structure of the tale accommodates its outward moving symbolic reference. An aspect of the symbolism that has remained relatively untouched is the extensive satire suggested by Jim Smiley's naming his bull-pup "Andrew Jackson" and his frog "Dan'l Webster." With this in mind, I wish to consider three questions: the degree to which there is a complexity of form in the story to sustain its social implications; the degree to which there is a secondary satire in the story to justify the inclusion of those implications; and the degree to which the satire implies a judgment of the East and West. To explore these questions is to see what Twain accomplished in bringing together the cream of the humor that preceded him. For his "Jumping Frog" blends the political satire perfected in Down East humor with the frame-work and oral techniques perfected in Old Southwestern humor.

Complex as the story is, the question of form—which has never been thoroughly described—is rather easily handled. To begin with, Twain has more than just a tale within a tale. He has in fact at least eight levels of story interest, each of which has several sides to it, so that the design better resembles a nest of boxes than it does a frame. There is 1. the story of the narrator's spoken and unspoken attitudes toward (a) the friend who wrote him from the East and lured him into a trap, toward (b) Simon Wheeler whom he regards as a garrulous simpleton, toward (c) Jim Smiley, the fabulous gambler, toward (d) the animals that Wheeler personalizes, and toward (e) the stranger who pulled a western trick on a Westerner and got away with it. Then there is 2. the story of Simon Wheeler's attitudes toward (a) the narrator and through him and his friend, toward (b) Easterners at large, toward (c) Jim Smiley, toward (d) the animals and toward (e) the stranger. Wheeler, moreover, represents 3. the western community at large that is continuously entertained by Smiley's antics. Also there are the attitudes of 4. the stranger, and of 5. Sam Clemens toward the various parties in his tale. Finally, we have the more restricted attitudes of 6. Smiley himself, which are confined to his animals and such persons as he can get to bet on them; and not the least significant attitudes are those of the animals themselves, particularly 7. the bull-pup and 8. the jumping frog.

At the level of story movement, the "Jumping Frog" has the same complexity as that of its multiple points of view. Twain employs an order of increasing detail and of ascending absurdity and fantasy. For example, after summary references to Smiley's willingness to bet "on anything that turned up" (a horse-race, dog-fight, cat-fight or chicken-fight), Wheeler tosses in two eccentric types of wager, one on which of "two birds setting on a fence . . . would fly first" and the second on Parson Walker's being the "best exhorter." These are paired with two other situations, each of which is given in greater detail, and the first of which (number three in the sequence) is absurd and fantastic—Smiley's willingness to follow a straddle bug to Mexico, if necessary, to find out its goal. The last member of the group is crashingly absurd, figuratively fantastic and practically insane, though, based on past performance, completely understandable, as Smiley, on hearing that the Parson's sick wife seems to be recovering, blurts out, "Well, I'll resk two-and-a-half she don't anyway."

In the grouping of mare, pup and frog, one proceeds from lesser to greater detail, complexity and surprise, but mainly from a lesser to a greater infusion of personality, one source of which is Smiley's hanging Jackson's name on the pup (which is connotatively apt) and Webster's on the frog (which is both connotatively *and* physically apt). Therein lies a considerable tale, for when such magisterial names are paired with the descriptions given these creatures, the reader has two of Twain's liveliest and most carefully developed burlesques. More of them in a moment. What should be noted here is the matter-of-factness of the impending satire, which deals with familiar history and can be called forth or not as the reader wishes, since, concurrently, there is so much else going on in the story.

The meshing of structure and satire in the interplay of eastern and western character traits may be seen not only in the sectional names given the animals, but, more obviously, in the various points of view, which polarize specifically eastern and western attitudes, in much the way that Webster and Jackson do. We rather guess that the stranger at the end is an Easterner, and this is borne out by Twain's subsequently having specifically labeled him a "Yankee" [in his "Private History of the 'Jumping Frog' Story"] . He is therefore an Easterner who plays the game of the Westerner and is specifically induced to play it on Smiley's terms, those, as Twain described Smiley, of a "wily Californian." Smiley is taken in by one of his own kind, and by a weakness—his avidity for gaming—induced by the wit which puts him into a class with the stranger. Moreover, as Twain recalled the original telling of the story (that is, original for him), he noted that the Westerners' major interest in it was in "the smartness of the stranger in taking in Smiley" and in his deep knowledge of a frog's nature for knowing that "a frog *likes* shot and is always ready to eat it." The stranger whets Smiley's appetite first by his curiosity (What's in the box? What's the frog good for?), then by his smugness ("I don't see no p'ints about that frog that's any better'n any other frog"), and further by the helpless innocence of his appeal for western hospitality ("the feller . . . says , kinder sadlike, 'Well, I'm only a stranger here, and I ain't got no frog. . . .' "). At the moment when the stranger is filling the frog, Twain gives us a glimpse of Smiley, out in the swamp, where he "slogged around in the mud for a long time." Being a humor character in the Jonsonian sense, Smiley was duped by his own single-mindedness.

In essence, then, the structure of the Jim Smiley story is that of a moral satire in the classical mold: Smiley's gambling fever led him to relinquish the normal protective xenophobia that guilefully motivated Simon Wheeler in the instructive tales he told about the guile that strangers might practice on simple Westerners.

To this exposure of simplicity in Smiley, Wheeler was an excellent foil. Furthermore, the relation of Wheeler to our narrator, "Mark Twain," recapitulates the structure of moral satire given in the relation of Smiley to the stranger and, with an even subtler grade of irony and one that renders the Smiley story itself ironic. Again the mounting complexity is based on characterization. This in part may be observed from what Twain did with Ben Coon of Angel's Camp, who inspired his sphinx-like Wheeler. Coon, according to Twain, was

a dull person, and ignorant; he had no gift as a storyteller, and no invention; in his mouth this espisode was merely history . . . he was entirely serious, for he was dealing with what to him were austere facts, and they interested him solely because they *were* facts; he was drawing on his memory, not his mind; he saw no humor in his tale, neither did his listeners; neither he nor they ever smiled or laughed; in my time I have not attended a more solemn conference.

If the tiresome earnestness of Coon was what first made the story "amusing" for Twain, in his retelling it, his own storyteller's earnestness is all ironic and "Mark Twain's" comments upon that earnestness made him a butt of the irony. We see more than our outside narrator, Twain, does in the fact that Wheeler "backed" him into a corner and "blockaded" him there with his chair, and *then* reeled off "the monotonous narrative." Wheeler is always several steps ahead of the narrator and never so many as when the narrator thinks him oblivious to the importance of what he relates.

He never smiled, he never frowned, he never changed his voice from the gentle-flowing key to which he tuned his initial sentence, he never betrayed the slightest suspicion of enthusiasm: but all through the interminable narrative there ran a vein of impressive earnestness and sincerity, which showed me plainly that, so far from his imagining that there was anything ridiculous or funny about his story, he regarded it as a really important matter, and admired its two heroes as men of transcendent genius in *finesse.*

Here is Ben Coon, but with a world of difference in the meaning attached to his seemingly obtuse incomprehension.

The moral satire comes clearly into focus when we see that Wheeler is to some extent the West getting its revenge for the trick of an Easterner, at the same time that he plays an instructive joke on the fastidious Mark Twain, a Westerner trying to outgrow his background in exchange for eastern respectability. His pretensions can be immediately ascertained from his looking down upon Wheeler, from the difference between his language and Wheeler's, and from his failure to see Wheeler's story as anything but long, tedious and useless. The fictive Twain thus stands somewhat in the relation to Wheeler that Smiley does to the stranger.

Twain so completely maintains perspective on his characters that no single attitude can be strictly assigned to him as author. Yet that very condition reflects something of the final complexity of his own personal point of view on the interrelation of eastern and western attitudes. He had shown in the story that neither was morally sufficient unto itself, but that one could strengthen the other attitude, which was the view he would come to both in his life and subsequent writing. The fact that for several years after writing it he could, on and off, approve and disapprove of the "Jumping Frog" indicates that he was at first uncertain of where he really stood on the sectional aspects of his story. Not only had he been embarrassed that a "villainous backwoods sketch" should represent him in the East; he was also disturbed that his wife-to-be might judge him by "that Jumping Frog book," with its distinctively western contents. However, when oral readings began to bring out the richness of his story, Twain recanted and told Livy he thought it "the best humorous sketch in America." The national reference signifies a triumph over sectionalism in his own attitudes, and a recognition that his tale contains both a criticism and a union of eastern and western values. That Twain was fully aware of the complexities of structure and attitude in his story is intimated by his remark to Livy that "a man might tell that Jumping Frog story fifty times without knowing *how* to tell it." For this reason, he went on, "I must read it in public some day, in order that people may know what there is in it."

The "Jumping Frog" assuredly does have a good deal more in it than usually meets the eye. Twain said that during one reading, "without altering a single word, it shortly [became] so absurd" that he had to laugh himself. Capital instances of the absurd were the sizable caricatures he had drawn of Andrew Jackson and Daniel Webster.

Twain did not name irrelevantly. Simon Wheeler was a free-wheeling yarn-spinner. Smiley, who was "uncommon lucky," had the perennial optimism of the gambler, which was the optimism of the West itself, and which also accounts for the superstitious naming of the pup and frog. In the pairing of the two animals, we get a western name pitted against an eastern one, a frontier democrat (supposedly) and National Republican against a Whig and spokesman for eastern capital. Added to this is the free and easy irreverence of the West indulging in one of its favorite democratic sports. Thus, Smiley's naming assumes a composite sectional and structural reference. On the one hand, actual correspondences between the animals and well-known traits of Jackson and Webster open up a considerable range of secondary meanings which are related to the basic story by their development of the East-West motif. On the other hand, the satire is functional. For while Twain seems to have been unacquainted with the earlier versions of his tale, he clearly had the imagination to recognize and exploit the vestigial ethos of its times, which Wheeler dates in the opening line of the internal story as "the winter of '49—or . . . spring of '50." In that context Smiley has the mood of a self-sufficient forty-niner; and as a means of dramatizing the assumptions of that mood, Twain endowed Smiley with the "Territory's" compensatory indifference to the values of the "States," specifically to the exalted associations of two high-ranking names in national politics. Indeed, Jackson and Webster were household gods for Smiley's generation, and for "old" Simon Wheeler's too. What better way for the western Adam to declare his worth than by smashing a few idols?

The events of the tale bring to mind some of the leading facts associated with the names of Jackson and Webster. Specifically, the bull-pup evokes the ironies of Jackson's reputation as a frontiersman, while the frog evokes the various flip-flops that characterized Webster's career. As the ironies surrounding Jackson are naturally different from those surrounding Webster, there are differences in the points Twain makes about them. However, with both men the central irony is that neither was what he seemed to have been.

Let us first consider Jackson and the bull-pup. For Wheeler to have had Jim Smiley casually compare his bull-pup with so stern a man as Jackson was to adopt the technique of insult used by the Whigs in Jackson's day when they associated him with the jackass. The technique was one of calculated insidiousness. Not only did the General not have the broad plebeian features of such animals as bulldogs and jackasses; he rather had the thinness, erect bearing and fine features of the true aristocrat that he prided himself on being. The nub of Twain's satire was that regardless of looks, it was how he acted and how he was thought of that counted; and

Jackson, of course, had become identified with political democracy despite himself, and even with frontier ruffianism and the devious opportunism of Simon Suggs.

In the pup's pugnacity, his combination of nonchalant confidence with tenacity in battle, his ferocity, his dependence on sheer will, his gambling spirit, his single-mindedness and iron nerve, as well as his having been "self-made," Twain's descriptions directly follow major aspects of Jackson's career. Like Smiley's dog, Old Hickory was the very image of toughness—to use the western idiom, he was just nothing but fight. But much of his actual fighting record was somewhat at variance with the idolatrous view of it. For example, his pointless victory at New Orleans was more the result of British mistakes than of his own military genius; while, staunch friend that he was of Aaron Burr's, Jackson the duelist had gained himself a name for rashness, brutality and peremptoriness, which was corroborated by his campaigns against the Creek and Seminole Indians, and his high-handed tactics in the Florida campaign of 1818, in which he had exceeded his orders. As for his famed truculence, outright brawling, frontier style, as in a dog-fight, was something the aristocratic Jackson—quite unlike Lincoln, for example—would not stoop to. In fact, one of the ironies of Jackson's association with frontiersmen was that while they had made him a celebrated commander, and while there was mutual affection between him and them, in his personal dealings, Jackson disdained to fight anyone of lower station. Nor was Jackson's "indomitable perseverance"—so perfectly symbolized by the bulldog's grip—an unmixed blessing. His tenacity in battle was often in reality a euphemism for his equally well-known "inflexity of purpose," which netted him a hollow victory in his biggest political battle, that with Nicholas Biddle over the United States Bank.

Twain's description of the pup touches on several aspects of Jackson's relationship to the frontier. Take the opening statement about the pup: "And he had a little small bull-pup, that to look at him you'd think he warn't worth a cent but to set around and look ornery and lay for a chance to steal something." With such a look as that, this pup might be Simon Suggs, Sut Lovingood, Thomas Jefferson Snodgrass or even Davy Crockett. However, his look is also an analogue of the legendary flashes of temper with which Jackson was known to have frightened opponents into submission. At the same time, the broad descriptive touches make this dog a caricature of the Jackson whom Whig cartoonists had ominously portrayed as an embodiment of the western frontier—that is just what the pup was meant to be.

Twain's second sentence about the bull-pup neatly captures the images in which the East and entrenched Whiggery at large viewed the specific threat of Jacksonism: "But as soon as the money was up on him he was a different dog; his under-jaw'd begin to stick out like the fo'castle of a steamboat, and his teeth would uncover and shine like the furnaces." In addition to its suggesting the fearful union of savagery with avarice, the idea that Smiley's pup has caught the gambling fever also carried a lurking reference to the stories of Jackson's fabulous exploits in gaming. Over and above other traits he shared with frontier gamblers, Jackson was exceedingly lucky, and in one well-known instance he helped his luck by adopting a special relationship with an animal he owned and bet on. Jackson's horse, Truxton, had the combined handicaps of Smiley's mare and pup; he ran as the underdog and with an injury. Disregarding the advice of friends who told him to pay the forfeit, Jackson was reported to have spoken to his horse, stroked his nose, and to have looked into his eyes as he would have into a man's; whereupon the horse responded by winning the first heat.

Twain's most incisive reflection on Jackson involves the manner of his having become a self-made man—a legend Twain explicitly satirized several years after writing the "Jumping Frog" [in an article for the Buffalo *Express,* May 1870]. Many of the eulogies on Jackson pictured him as a man who had been "born . . . of poor, but respectable parents" and had achieved greatness "by no other means than the energy of his character." *Character,* in Jackson's case, invariably meant "obduracy and vehemence of will." In eulogizing the bull-pup, Wheeler gave a more meaningful account of character. He lamented that despite the inner quality of the dog ("it was a good pup"; "the stuff was in him"; he had "genius"), this Andrew Jackson had not had the chance to make a name for himself. In his last fight, seeing "how he'd been imposed on" by Smiley's mania for garish betting situations, the dog

give Smiley a look, as much as to say his heart was broke, and it was *his* fault . . . and then he limped off a piece and laid down and died. It was a good pup, was that Andrew Jackson, and would have made a name for hisself if he'd lived, for the stuff was in him and he had genius—I know it, because he hadn't no opportunities to speak of, and it don't stand to reason that a dog could make such a fight as he could under them circumstances if he hadn't no talent.

The crucial, and often repeated, question about Jackson's rise to eminence had been raised rather early in his career when Samuel Putnam Waldo inquired, "If he had not talents and virtues, would he not have remained in obscurity?" Twain gave that question an ironic treatment, when, using the same terminology and reasoning, he had Wheeler emphasize opportunity as the instrument of success for persons naturally endowed with talent and goodness.

If ferocity and iron will had made a bulldog of Jackson, the political turnabouts, the desire for pacification and harmony, plus an overall jelly-like softness were even more impressively the Websterian qualities suggested by Smiley's frog. While Jackson in no wise looked like the pup, Webster did resemble the frog. He had the protuberant belly, the length of nose, the black eyes, the high cheek bones and downward sloping face; and, of course, as a speaker, he had both the mouth and the wind of a frog as well as his deep intonation of voice. As politician, he could also display the frog's inscrutable placidity of mien. By such references as those to the frog's flopping down on the floor "solid as a gob of mud," to his being "solid as an anvil" (which in revision became a "church"), to his being "anchored out," and to his looking "mighty baggy" with the shot in him, Twain underscored the staunch Whiggery and solidity of character that had gilded Webster's reputation, while each reference equally implies stodginess and like pejoratives. The frog's jumping was everything, though, for through it Twain illustrated the combination of lumpish conservatism with the hectic, often slippery, politicking that were in reality the alpha and omega of Webster's accomplishment.

Closely allied to jumping are the matters of education and worth, which are its aims. On catching his frog, Smiley "cal'lated to educate him," and he did nothing for three months but "learn that frog to jump." This was more than a superfluous improvement on nature; for with the frog as much as with Webster, jumping was the triumph of an education that brought out what each was most gifted at. A ready learner, Webster developed the highest facility for moving from less to more convenient political positions. Still, for all his education, Webster was five times unsuccessful in capturing his party's presidential nomination, losing to some very ordinary, and, as he thought, unqualified candidates like Generals William Henry Harrison in 1840 and Winfield Scott in 1852. It was really as if the party had looked him over and found no points about Webster that made him any better than any other candidate.

But, fortunately for a man who had made a career of jumping, disappointments came as a challenge to his mobility. In fact, the politician's sense of numerous alternatives parallels the Westerner's sense of the vast opportunities afforded by the frontier. Since Webster's one unwavering motive had been to protect the New England business community, no small part of his role was to make the difficult jump or straddle, and, with froglike complacency, not let on that he had overly exerted himself. Additionally, Webster had an intense desire to enrich himself and to seem a man of moral worth.

Keeping in mind, then, the relevance to Webster of such matters as appearance, conservatism, education, jumping, complacency, cupidity and worth, one needs only to re-read the first paragraph about Smiley's frog to see how completely Twain had *done* Webster in almost every characterizing detail—as in the following:

> . . . He'd give him a little punch behind, and the next minute you'd see that frog whirling in the air like a doughnut—see him turn one summer-set, or maybe a couple, if he got a good start, and come down flat-footed and all right, like a cat. . . . Smiley said all a frog wanted was education, and he could do 'most anything—and I believe him. Why, I've seen him set Dan'l Webster down here on this floor . . . and sing out, "Flies, Dan'l, flies!" and quicker'n you could wink he'd spring straight up and snake a fly off'n the counter there and flop down on the floor ag'in as solid as a gob of mud, and fall to scratching the side of his head with his hind foot as indifferent as if he hadn't no idea he'd been doin' any more'n any frog might do. You never see a frog so modest and straightfor'ard as he was, for all he was so gifted. And when it come to fair and square jumping on a deal level, he could get over more ground at one straddle than any animal of his breed you ever see. . . . Smiley would ante up money on him as long as he had a red. Smiley was monstrous proud of his frog, . . . for fellers that had traveled and been everywheres all said he laid over any frog that ever they see (p. 4).

To know the extent to which the frog's vaunted jumps—as well as his crucial failure to jump—form a compound satire on Webster's favorite maneuver, one need only refamiliarize oneself with the salient points in his record.

One gets a fairly good sample of his dexterity in a few of the jumps inspired by Jackson, whose name alone gave the arch Whig more than one punch from behind. For example, when he heard that Jackson was prepared to use force if necessary to prevent southern states from nullifying disagreeable aspects of the Tariff of 1828, Webster at first objected, and then went over to Jackson's side. Just prior to this, Webster had bitterly opposed Jackson's veto of the bill for rechartering the United States Bank. But that position had not been completely firm, for when Jackson took action against the Bank, Webster was hesitant as to how he should react. He had every reason to support the Bank, but was reluctant to join Clay and Calhoun in its defense because he had been exposing them too recently as enemies of the Republic, and would have to condemn Executive interference with the Bank, after he had just approved Executive interference with the interests of South Carolina.

What was true of Webster's relationship to Jackson was true of his career as a whole. Richard Current [in *Daniel Webster and the Rise of National Conservatism*] probably understated his facility when he indicated that Webster "was to spend the better part of his long career in defending principles he had attacked and condemning others he had opposed during his apprentice years." The frequency of Webster's tergiversation placed him on both sides of every major issue of his time—free trade, protectionism, monopolies, nullification, states rights, the sale of public lands, executive authority, Unionism, the nonexpansion of slavery and the enforcement of the Fugitive Slave Law. As with Smiley's frog, the very breadth of Webster's straddles gave promise of an ability that would be belied by his performance in crucial tests. When a combination of northern businessmen and southern planters envisioned the possibility of running him on a bipartisan Unionist ticket in 1852, Webster responded by refusing to jump when pressed by friends not to desert the Whigs, and then by jumping in his very refusal to do so by stating that he knew the people would not elect General Scott, and that he himself would vote for his New Hampshire neighbor Franklin Pierce.

From all that one can tell, Twain's private opinions of Jackson and Webster were in some respects similar to those that emerge from the story and in others significantly different from them. He growled about Jackson's responsibility for the practice of using civil service for patronage, and he wished that the Battle of New Orleans had not been fought, so that the nation might have been spared the "harms" of Jackson's presidency. On the other hand, Twain did not let his affinity for Whiggish ideas interfere with his dislike of Webster, whose love letters struck him as "diffuse, conceited, 'eloquent,' [and] bathotic" and who was identified in his mind with the moralizing and empty rhetoric he burlesqued in schoolgirl compositions. With respect to the "Jumping Frog," though Twain's political antipathy toward Jackson exceeded his literary antipathy toward Webster, the character and actions of the bull-pup have much more to recommend them than do the comparable aspects of the frog. Clearly, one reason why the story favors Jackson over Webster, despite the satire on *both* men, is the predominance of Simon Wheeler's point of view over others in the story. What happens, therefore, is that Wheeler's point of view permits Twain to eat his cake and have it: to vent his prejudices in the subsidiary satire and to maintain an artistic objectivity in the primary context of his story.

Twain's use of sectional values likewise reflects a coalescence of external comment (satire) with internal necessity (art). If he seems to favor the West over the East, sectional values are obviously mixed in the un-eastern credulity of the gentleman narrator and in the wryly un-western moral (beware of a stranger) of the frog anecdote. Ultimately, the ideal suggested by Twain's modification of eastern and western attitudes, seems to require a blending of the Whiggish paragon of the self-made man with the realization of it achieved by an Andrew Jackson in the unfettered conditions of the frontier.

JAMES M. COX

THE STRUCTURE OF "THE JUMPING FROG"

Simon Wheeler was, after all, Mark Twain's chief means of transforming the story into art, for in its original form the Jumping Frog story was no more than a crude account of a practical joke in which one gambler takes the measure of another.

Mark Twain did not change the original joke so much as he enfolded it in the consciousness—which is to say the *style*—of Simon Wheeler. Thus, as everyone knows, the greatness of "The Jumping Frog" is in its telling, in the creation of a powerful illusion that the story is being told instead of written. In the classic Henry James or Hawthorne story the illusion that the story is being told by a narrator drops away because the narrator's consciousness is so urbanely literary. The same is true in Washington Irving's sketches. But in "The Jumping Frog," the fact that the story is written—in the earliest version the story was an epistle addressed to Artemus Ward—is lost amid the sound of Wheeler's voice. The illusion of the story's being told is produced by Mark Twain's use of two narrators: one, "Mark Twain," who uses literary or written language in the frame around the story; the other, Wheeler, who counters with the nonliterary or spoken language, the dialect.

Such a structure, instead of recalling the urbane sketch which Irving perfected, rises out of the traditions developed by Southwestern humorists. By means of fully styled literary frames, such artists—and they were artists—as A. B. Longstreet, Thomas Bangs Thorpe, Johnson J. Hooper, and George W. Harris were able to condescend to the dialect they skillfully mimicked. The truth of their form lay in their adherence to the very class distinctions their form mirrored. Thus they were to a man, as Kenneth Lynn has wisely observed, Whigs in politics who felt no egalitarian guilt in treating dialect characters as the bumpkins, gulls, rogues, and low comedy characters the superior literary language defined them to be. To be sure, there is a cruelty in the humor of Longstreet, Hooper, and Harris, but there is not the sentimentality which characterizes the work of such literary exploiters of dialect as Cooper and Harriet Beecher Stowe. For although both Cooper and Mrs. Stowe tried to use dialect, in the very act of asserting the "nobility" of dialect characters, they invariable relied upon literary language for analysis and "elevated" description. Thus their dialect could convey only picturesque utterance and quaint or crackerbarrel rural identities, at best giving conventional wisdom a fresh turn. Southwestern humorists, on the other hand, being freed of a sentiment which contradicted their form, were able to discover much more vitality in their humorous creations. At their best, as in Harris' Sut Lovingood, the dialect becomes so extreme that it threatens to be a language in itself; or in Thorpe's "The Big Bear of Arkansas," the frontier hunter's story of the legendary bear becomes the vehicle for disclosures at once broadly—even crudely—humorous and strikingly imaginative.

The form of "The Jumping Frog," like that of "The Big Bear of Arkansas," sets the oral story inside a literary frame. But unlike Thorpe, Mark Twain never interrupts Wheeler's story once it begins, until the very end of the sketch. And whereas the nub of Thorpe's story covertly revolves around the old masculine joke of being caught with one's breeches down—the hunter is surprised by the looming bear at the inopportune moment of his morning defecation—Mark Twain's humor is open and utterly innocent in this respect.

It is, in fact, Wheeler's total innocence which sets him apart from Thorpe's bragging and freewheeling frontiersman. Thus Mark Twain, the literary narrator, consciously and overtly describes Wheeler's manner and method of narration:

He never smiled, he never frowned, he never changed his voice from the gentle-flowing key to which he tuned his initial sentence, he never betrayed the slightest suspicion of enthusiasm; but all through the interminable narrative there ran a vein of impressive earnestness and sincerity, which showed me plainly that, so far from his imagining that there was anything ridiculous or funny about his story, he regarded it as a really important matter, and admired its two heroes as men of transcendent genius in *finesse.* I let him go on in his own way, and never interrupted him once (pp. 1-2).

While Mark Twain painfully condescends to suffer the boredom of listening to Wheeler's interminable narrative, Wheeler is apparently so absorbed in his own story that he is utterly unaware of his listener's attitude. He is, after all, the deadpan narrator; and if he suspects the condescension, he betrays no hint of his suspicion, being content to blockade Mark Twain and force him to undergo the role of listener.

This structure, revealing two contrasting styles, imitates the action of Wheeler's story. Smiley, who had consciously trained his animals, fostering their genius and lying in wait for gullible souls willing to bet on the merely natural animals to beat them, is "taken in" by a deadpan stranger.

Innocently refusing to see the virtue of Smiley's frog, the mysterious stranger dupes him into fetching a mere ordinary, unpedigreed, and unnamed frog with which he defeats the celebrated Dan'l Webster. The stranger is not innocent, of course, but the first of a long line of mock-innocents to people Mark Twain's world, and his victory over Smiley comes by virtue of his having weighted Dan'l Webster with so much bird-shot that the frog's incomparable style is reduced to no more than an impotent strain against its recently acquired sense of gravity. The stranger's secret act of "fixing" the jumping contest corresponds to the artist's "secret" structure which becomes apparent to the reader only after he has been taken in.

In much the same way that the stranger's deadpan takes in Smiley, Wheeler's style is "taking in" the literary language which introduces it. The literary "Mark Twain" quite appropriately suspects that he has been taken in as he recounts the story, but he obtusely attributes the trick to his friend from the remote East, not to the beguiling Wheeler. Yet it would be a distortion to attribute a sly trickery to Wheeler. He is no mere Western confidence man taking his revenge on the superior Easterner. Such an interpretation reduces the story to the familiar East-versus-West regionalism, which is precisely the dimension "The Jumping Frog" at once exploited and transcended. The comic force of the story lies in the unwitting collaboration between the two narrators, and the impossibility of being sure of Wheeler's deadpan. The literary narrator is bored and abruptly interrupts the inveterate Wheeler who is about to launch into another anecdotal episode concerning the unforgettable Smiley. Wheeler presumably neither recognizes nor resents the condescension. He betrays no suspicion, and the reader who would have him guileful must read in his own distrust, for Wheeler apparently moves forward in serene oblivion. His obliviousness, his total self-absorption, both defines his character and constitutes his humor. Brooding over the decaying mining camp almost like a tutelary deity, Wheeler's memory, moving irresistibly backward in an associative recovery of the past, converts all the speculation, deception, and disillusion in the very scene of the mining camp into the rich recollection of Jim Smiley and his frog.

The full force of that conversion lies in the astonishing fullness of Wheeler's memory, which yields a return far exceeding the mere necessity of the tale he recalls. Wheeler's invariable digressions constitute the excess of pleasure his remarkable narrative produces. Take for example the description of Smiley's dog, a gratuitous miracle that the apparently absent-minded Wheeler can't help remembering:

And he had a little small bull-pup, that to look at him you'd think he warn't worth a cent but to set around and look ornery and lay for a chance to steal something. But as soon as money was up on him he was a different dog; his under-jaw'd begin to stick out like the fo'castle of a steamboat, and his teeth would uncover and shine like the furnaces. And a dog might tackle him and bully-rag him, and bite him, and throw him over his shoulder two or three times, and Andrew Jackson—which was the name of the pup—Andrew Jackson would never let on but what he was satisfied, and hadn't expected nothing else—and the bets being doubled and doubled on the other side all the time, till the money was all up; and then all of a sudden he would grab that other dog jest by the j'int of his hind leg and freeze to it—not chaw, you understand, but only just grip and hang on till they throwed up the sponge, if it was a year. Smiley always come out winner on that pup, till he harnessed a dog once that didn't have no hind legs, because they'd been sawed off in a circular saw, and when the thing had gone along far enough, and the money was all up, and he come to make a snatch for his pet holt, he see in a minute how he'd been imposed on, and how the other dog had him in the door, so to speak, and he 'peared suprised, and then he looked sorter discouraged-like, and didn't try no more to win the fight, and so he got shucked out bad. He give Smiley a look, as much as to say his heart was broke, and it was *his* fault, for putting up a dog that hadn't no hind legs for him to take holt of, which was his main dependence in a fight, and then he limped off a piece and laid him down and died. It was a good pup, was that Andrew Jackson, and would have made a name for hisself if he'd lived, for the stuff was in him and he had genius—I know it, because he hand't no opportunities to speak of, and it don't stand to reason that a dog could make such a fight as he could under them circumstances if he hadn't no talent. It always makes me feel sorry when I think of that last fight of his'n, and the way it turned out (p. 3).

Here the speaker's similes and metaphors—his comparison of the dog with a steamboat, and his description of the dog "freezing" to his victim—not only reveal an easy appropriation of diverse experiences; the sustained commitment with which he "humanizes" the dog reveals the capacity and intensity of his investment in the experience he narrates. This investment executes the superb humorous reversal, making Andrew Jackson and not the two-legged dog the object of sympathy, and in the very process converting the clichés of sympathy into a transcendent humorous synthesis.

The character of Wheeler provided both the style and structure for Mark Twain's first masterpiece. Wheeler was as essential to the humor of the sketch as "Mark Twain" was to Samuel Clemens. His grave and pained earnestness, the equivalent in narrative to Mark Twain's deadpan on the lecture platform, was the very embodiment of the humorist's version of the original seriousness from which the tale originated. His voice in the story seems interminable because Mark Twain's interruption of that voice, which constitutes the end of the story, creates the illusion that the voice goes on forever. Mark Twain himself evidently thought that it continued, for he attempted at later times to call on Wheeler again, but never successfully. The reason was that Simon Wheeler had said all he could say—all he *had* to say. The virtue of the ending lay in preserving the illusion that Wheeler was long-winded and endlessly digressive when in reality the tale he tells is a masterpiece of compression and economy.

Given such a discovery, Samuel Clemens could well feel that his humorous career had fatally begun. To his brother Orion he wrote on October 19, 1865—almost immediately after he had completed "The Jumping Frog" but before it was published—what is one of his most important letters. Beginning with that heightened gravity faintly suggesting parody, he declared that Orion had the genius for preaching. As for himself, he had had two powerful ambitions—to be a pilot and to be a preacher. One he had realized, but the other had eluded him because of his deficiency of religion. Orion, he confidently declared, should leave the pursuit of law and yield to the prompting of his true genius. He himself had accepted his own call:

I *have* had a "call" to literature, of a low order—i.e. humorous. It is nothing to be proud of, but it is my strongest suit, & if I were to listen to that maxim of stern *duty* which says that to do right you *must* multiply the one or the two or the three talents which the Almighty entrusts to your keeping. I would long ago have ceased to meddle with things for which I was by nature unfitted & turned my attention to seriously scribbling to excite the *laughter* of God's creatures. Poor, pitiful business! Though the Almighty did His part by me—for the talent is a mighty engine when supplied with the steam of *education*—which I have not got, & so its pistons & cylinders & shafts move feebly & for a holiday show & are useless for any good purpose.

To excite the laughter of God's creatures! That is the unmistakable intention shining through the assumed stateliness, the ponderous gravity, the elaborate mechanical analogy, and the pervasive self-depreciation. It does not merely shine through but assimilates these solemnities in such a way that they become part of the intention itself. This conversion, mirroring Samuel Clemens' conversion from would-be preacher to low humorist, was both the act and fate to which he would give his life.

3

A TRUE STORY

After becoming nationally famous as the Wild Humorist of the West, Mark Twain moved to the East where he married a genteel young woman named Olivia Langdon and (with the financial assistance of her wealthy father) became established in respectable society as the editor of the Buffalo *Express*. Aspiring to become known not merely as a journalist but as a member of the literati, he moved his family in 1872 into an imposing mansion in Hartford, Connecticut, in a neighborhood inhabited by many successful authors of the day. When one of his stories was accepted for publication by the highly regarded *Atlantic Monthly*, he felt he had at last arrived.

His first of many contributions to the *Atlantic* came out in December of 1874, entitled "A True Story, Repeated Word for Word as I Heard It." Twain, of course, did more than simply transcribe the tale as the title suggests, but the incidents recorded are true. The Aunt Rachel of the story was Auntie Cord, cook at Quarry Farm where the Clemens family often summered. A former slave, she took pride in having once brought $1,000 when sold at auction. William Dean Howells, editor of the *Atlantic,* paid his new author the extravagent sum of sixty dollars for the three-page piece. Much later, reminiscing about his years as editor, Howells mentioned several prominent Western contributors to the magazine, warming up for his favorite:

Later came Mark Twain, originally of Missouri, but then provisionally of Hartford, and now ultimately of the solar system, not to say of the universe. He came first with "A True Story," one of those noble pieces of humanity with which the South has atoned chiefly, if not solely, through him for all its despite to the negro.

Critics have continued to admire the story ever since, but it has never been widely anthologized and thus has failed to receive the attention that Twain's more popular short pieces have enjoyed.

PHILIP FONER
"A TRUE STORY"

Reviewing *Sketches Old and New* by Mark Twain, William Dean Howells wrote in the *Atlantic Monthly* of December, 1875: "by far the most perfect piece of work in the book is 'A True Story' . . . . The rugged truth of the sketch leaves all other stories of slave life infinitely far behind, and reveals a gift in the author for the simple, dramatic report of reality which we have seen equalled in no other American writer." Every reader of "A True Story" will agree with Howell's evaluation. It is truly a masterpiece.

* * * * * * * *

In but a few pages, Twain tells us more about the Negro people, the true nature of slavery, the Civil War, the role of the Negro people in that conflict, than is achieved in many volumes. He makes clearly evident: (1) The dignity of the Negro woman; (2) That to characterize the Negro people as fun-loving children who have no real concerns or problems of importance is a canard; (3) The love of the Negro family—of the Negro slave husband and wife for each other, the Negro slave mother for her children; (4) The hideous nature of slavery, that tears families apart; (5) The desertion of their plantations by the slaveowners, leaving the slaves to shift for themselves; (6) The liberating role of the Union army; (7) The devotion of the Negro slaves to the Union army, and their eagerness to aid the Union soldiers; (8) The role of the Negro people in fighting for their own liberation by participation in the Union army by military and other service; (9) The sympathy of the Union officers for the slave woman, revealing the significance of the entrance of the Union army into the South; (10) The search of the son for his mother as typifying what took place during and after the Civil War as thousands of former slaves moved about the South looking to reunite their families, separated during slavery.

From *Mark Twain: Social Critic* (New York: International Publishers, 1958), pp. 202, 204. Reprinted by the permission of the publisher.

GERALD J. FENGER
TELLING IT LIKE IT WAS

Twain "tells it like it was" in one of his finest stories, aptly titled "A True Story." First published as "A True Story, Repeated Word for Word as I Heard It" in the *Atlantic Monthly* issue of November, 1874, this moving story, as Justin Kaplan has noted, foreshadows *Huckleberry Finn* "in its explicit sympathy for the Negro, its level vision of the brutalities of a slaveholding society," and in "the enormous skill" Twain "displays in telling a first-person story in impeccably nuanced but never obscure dialect."

Though he used a small frame device to set the scene for her, Twain allowed "Aunt Rachel" to tell her own story to "Misto C———" (ostensibly Clemens). In the course of her chronicle she emerges as one of his most rounded character creations, living up to the expectations derived from her description:

She was of mighty frame and stature; she was sixty years old, but her eye was undimmed and her strength unabated. She was a cheerful, hearty soul, and it was no more trouble for her to laugh than it is for a bird to sing (94).

Aunt Rachel was prompted to tell her story when "Mister C," having watched her emit peal after peal of laughter when teased, asked her, "Aunt Rachel, how is it that you've lived sixty years and never had any trouble?" (94). This question sobered her instantly, and she earnestly replied, "Has I had any trouble? Misto C———, I's gwyne to tell you, den I leave it to you" (95).

And so she did. She told how she was separated from her family, her husband and seven children, at a slave auction. Her favorite child, little Henry, later ran off to the North, became a barber, and when the Civil War started he sold his business and began searching for his mother. Twenty-two years after her separation from her family, Rachel's master ran away, from the advancing union armies, and she was re-united with her son, whom she discovered among a group of Negro soldiers who had come to have a party in the kitchen of her former master's house.

Satire directed against white bigots is evident when early in her narration Rachel announced that she loved her children, even though they

---

From an unpublished dissertation, *Perspectives of Satire in Mark Twain's Short Stories* (Texas Christian University, 1974), pp. 113-118. Printed by permission of the author (title is editor's).

were black: "Dey was black, but de Lord can't make no chil'en so black but what dey mother loves 'em an' wouldn't give 'em up, no, not for anything dat's in dis whole world" (95). This speech foreshadows Huck Finn's musings on the same subject. He had observed the Negroes' love of their children, a phenomenon which his white education had apparently taught him was not possible, for blacks were something other than human. Nevertheless, Huck had *seen* it for himself in Jim's love and yearning for his lost family, and he could only remark, "'Tain't natural, but I guess it's so."

The most memorable portion of Aunt Rachel's account is, doubtless, her description of being cruelly separated from her family when all of them are sold at the slave auction in Richmond, a move made necessary by the financial distress of their mistress:

Dey put chains on us an' put us on a stan' as high as dis po'ch—twenty feet high—an' all de people stood aroun', crowds an' crowds. An dey'd come up dah an' look at us all roun', an' squeeze our arm, an make us git up an' walk, an' den say, 'Dis one too ole,' or 'Dis one lame,' or 'Dis one don't 'mount to much.' An' day sole my ole man, an' took him away, an' dey begin to sell my chil'en an' take dem away, an' I begin to cry; an' de man say, 'Shet up yo' damn blubberin',' an' hit me on de mouf wid his han' (96).

She went on to tell how her entire family was sold, and how she tried to save her youngest, little Henry. She grabbed him and held him tightly, but they pulled him away from her. She fought fiercely, beating the men on the head with her chain, and they beat her in return, but her efforts were to no avail. She was never again to see her husband or any of her seven children except Henry.

Though Aunt Rachel's story is a sorrowful one, Twain saves it from degenerating into a maudlin morass by the masterful way he allows her to tell it. She is, to be sure, a person to be pitied, but she is also a humorous person because of the manner in which she tells her tale of woe. Her expressions, for example, reveal her to be a story-teller of great verve and gusto, one who prompts a chuckle, or at least a smile now and then along the way. Expletives abound: "My lan'! . . . My souls! . . . mine I *tell* you!" In describing her anger at having her kitchen taken over by a group of frolicking, black union soldiers, she says:

. . . I was just a bilin'! Mad? I was just a-boomin'! I swelled aroun!, and swelled aroun'; I was just a-itchin' for 'em to do somefin' for to start me . . . . De res' o' de niggers go to laughin', an' den my sould *alive* but I was hot! My eye was just a-blazin'! (97).

One of her favorite exclamations, borrowed from her mother, has to be billed as a striking, unusual, and funny expression: "I wa'n't bawn in de mash to be fool' by trash. I's one o' de old Blue Hen's Chickens, *I* is!" Translated, this means that she is no common, ordinary black: she was born in Maryland, and she was mighty proud of it! (Rachel was not actually born in Maryland, but her mother was, and her mother used to say these words frequently. Rachel, naturally, started using them to good advantage whenever she was riled.)

Following her discovery of her son's identity—"De Lord God ob heaven be praise', I got my own ag'in!" (98)—Twain brings her story to an abrupt close with a memorable, ironic line: "Oh no, Misto C———, I hain't had no trouble. An' no *joy!*" (98). The frame narrator does not intrude again. Aunt Rachel had obviously encountered *both* trouble and joy in her life; but far more trouble than "Mister C———" had ever imagined.

"Mister C———" (Twain) also apparently failed to perceive the value of "A True Story" and even neglected to acknowledge the humor in the tale he created. When he submitted the story to William Dean Howells as his first contribution to the *Atlantic Monthly,* Twain seemed reticent and apologetic. He wrote: "I enclose also a 'True Story' which has no humor in it. You can pay as lightly as you choose for that, for it is rather out of my line." "I've kept the 'True Story',", Howells replied, "which I think extremely good and touching and with the best and reallest kind of black talk in it." Thirteen months later, in the *Atlantic* for December of 1875, Howells published a review of Twain's *Sketches New and Old* and [according to Kaplan] mentioned that

. . . some readers had been puzzled by the seriousness of "A True Story" and had feared a "lurking joke in it." His own seasoned judgement was: "The rugged truth of the sketch leaves all other stories of slave life infinitely far behind, and reveals a gift in the author for the simple, dramatic report of reality which we have seen equalled in no other American writer."

Howells was not far from the truth, for the story was excellently told, and, perhaps, in the subject matter which it treats, exceeded in Twain's canon only by *Pudd'nhead Wilson* and *Huckleberry Finn.* Twain's best work, as we have seen, often occurs in his short pieces, and "A True Story" certainly is one of his best tales. Aunt Rachel is one of the most noble characters Twain ever created. Anyone who could endure what she did and still emerge with such a sane, healthy, and even happy attitude has to possess a large portion of what Maynard Mack calls the qualities of the true hero. She is more than a good plain person; she has suffered much of man's inhumanity to man, and it has not broken her nor made her cynical. It has made her superior to the mass of men—able to laugh at man's folly and to give the appearance of never having had any trouble in six decades of living. She tells her own story with such intensity of feeling that the reader is compelled to accept its truth and to sympathize with her. Her final statement is bitterly ironic. She had had much trouble in life, but she is still able to experience joy. A story as powerful as hers could only be told in the first-person—in her own accents that mirror the pathos of her life.

WILLIAM GIBSON

THE ARTISTRY OF "A TRUE STORY"

By the time Twain conceived and composed "A True Story, Repeated Word for Word as I Heard It" for the *Atlantic* in 1874, he had passed through his apprenticeship and could bring to bear on Aunt Cord's telling of certain great events in her life his knowledge of the formal-colloquial frame story, the potential of the vernacular for effects of pathos as well as humor, and certain small but effective actions performed as though on the stage.

The immediate inspiration for this first Mark Twain piece to be published in the prestigious *Atlantic Monthly* was the history of Auntie Cord, the cook at Quarry Farm in Elmira, who had been "in slavery more than forty years." As he explained to Howells, he had first *told* the yarn to John Hay and some others; they had liked it; he then decided to *write* it. As for his repeating the tale "Word for Word as I Heard It," this can scarcely be literally true. He said, "I have not altered the old colored woman's story except to begin it at the beginning, instead of the middle, as she did—& traveled both ways." The intent of the subtitle is plainly to claim the status of history rather than fiction for the story, and perhaps to warn the reader not to expect humor as its central feature.

The illusion of biography or private history is created at once by the subtitle and by the unusual reference to the "I" introducer of the tale as "Misto C———"; yet the creative or fictive touch appears immediately in the renaming of the real Auntie Cord as "Aunt Rachel." What echoes

From *The Art of Mark Twain* (New York: Oxford University Press, 1976), pp. 76–79, and reprinted by permission (title is editor's).

resonated in the name "Rachel" for Clemens—as for Melville [in *Moby Dick*]: "Lamentation & bitter weeping; Rachel weeping for her children refused to be comforted for her children, because they were not."

The stout cook, Aunt Rachel, so jolly, so fond of laughter, so willing to be chaffed, suddenly turns sober at the thoughtless question from "Misto C———": "How is it that you've lived sixty years and never had any trouble?" Her answer to the question, "Has I had any trouble?" is in effect the drama and the story. She begins by telling of her relative happiness, in slavery in Virginia, with her husband and their seven children, her little Henry's scarring his head and wrist, and her boast (like mother's) that she is a Marylander, "one o' de ole Blue Hen's Chickens" (p. 95). She then recounts her pain and misery as her family is sold at auction in Richmond, and her fierce resistance when her youngest is taken from her, and his whispering to her that he will run away and work and buy her freedom. With the opening of the Civil War Aunt Rachel becomes cook for a group of Union officers in a big headquarters house, and often asks them about her son, just as (she learns later) he has been searching for her, while servant to a Union colonel. This managing of essential fact in their twenty-two year separation leads of course to the long-delayed and very moving recognition of mother and son. Henry is part of a *"nigger* ridgment*"* on guard at headquarters, and at a dancing party in her big kitchen overhears her scold the laughing young black dancers: "I wa'n't bawn in de mash to be fool' by trash! I's one o' de old Blue Hen's Chickens, I is!" He cannot sleep thereafter. And when he returns to the kitchen early in the morning, Aunt Rachel looks into his face, finds the scars on wrist and forehead, and cries, "If you an't my Henry, what is you doin' wid dis welt on yo' wris' an' dat sk-yar on yo' forehead? De Lord God ob heaven be praise', I got my own ag'in!" Aunt Rachel then returns to the original question, saying "Oh no, Misto C———, I hain't had no trouble. An' no *joy!*" (pp. 97-98).

The transformation of Aunt Rachel from conventional Negro cook and servant to a pathetic and intensely individualized heroine takes place quickly. When the yarn begins, she is seated at twilight on the porch steps of the farmhouse below her employers, as befits a servant. Then (as she warms to her story) she had gradually risen, and "now she towered above us, black against the stars." At the end, she re-enacts the discovery of her son's identity with intense physical immediacy, and pushes back the hair and the sleeve of "Misto C———" just as, she says, she had done with Henry (p. 98). The whole sketch is thus rendered dramatic through its dialogue and its slight but revelatory actions. A final dimension, like the name Rachel, emerges in parallels to an old spiritual that was surely in Clemens's mind when he was writing the story—"Nobody Knows deh

Trouble I've Seen." The singer mourns, "Sometimes I'm up, sometimes I'm down/Oh, yes, Lord/Sometimes my head's bowed to the ground/Oh, yes, Lord," voicing directly what Aunt Rachel feels in reviewing *her* troubles. The conclusion of the spiritual, too—"Glory, Hallelujah"—is a cry of acceptance very close to Aunt Rachel's quiet, understated assertion, "I hain't had no trouble. An' no *joy!*" The Hartford housemaid Katy Leary testified that one moonlight night at the Charles Dudley Warner house, "Mr. Clemens" sang spirituals and became lost in his singing:

> He put his two hands up to his head, just as though all the sorrow of them negroes was upon him; and then he begun to sing, "Nobody Knows the Trouble I Got, Nobody Knows but Jesus." That was one of them negro spirituals songs, and when he come to the end, to the Glory Halleluiah, he gave a great shout—just like the negroes do—he shouted out the Glory, Glory, Halleluiah!

Aunt Rachel gains stature by association with the biblical Rachel and the anonymous singer of "Nobody Knows deh Trouble I've Seen." Yet she is unsentimentally drawn, a recognizably flawed human being, in that she is proud of her Maryland ancestry and contemptuous of slaves who are "trash" because they were "bawn in the mash"—that is, in the cattlefood bin of a barn. She naively thinks of her boy Henry as still a child rather than the grown man he has become. She suffers and is angered by the laughter of the "spruce young nigger" and the "yaller wench" who find her red turban funny. But she knows what she is *for*—she is a cook—and she is as courageous as she is loving, beating the auctioneer's men over the head with her chain when they take Henry forcibly from her.

Recognition of the quality of Mark Twain's story came immediately from the Civil War veteran and writer, J. W. DeForest. Shortly after the tale appeared, the author of *Miss Ravenel's Conversion from Secession to Loyalty* (1867) wrote to Howells: "By the way, tell Mark Twain to try pathos now & then. His 'True Story,'—the story of the old negress,—was a really great thing, amazingly natural & humorous, & touching even to the drawing of tears." What his editor thought of it is implicit in the fact that the *Atlantic* sent the author twenty dollars a page for it—the highest rate ever paid to any of its contributors.

4

THE FACTS CONCERNING
THE RECENT CARNIVAL OF CRIME
IN CONNECTICUT

Twain's career was flourishing when he wrote "The Carnival of Crime."
First published in the *Atlantic,* June 1876 (the same year that *Tom
Sawyer* appeared), the story was six years later included in the collection
entitled *The Stolen White Elephant, Etc.* Even though written in happy
times, the story perhaps (as Maxwell Geismar suggests at the end of the
first selection in this section) presages "certain strains in Eden." Although
Twain was enjoying an immense income from book royalties, lecture
tours, and magazine articles, his expenses spiraled astronomically at the
grand Hartford mansion. And although he relished being feted and
admired, the glittering social whirl was both exhausting and time consuming. He escaped finally by taking his family to Europe where he hoped
to curb expenses and find the privacy needed for work and rest.

The story details an audacious fantasy in which a first-person narrator
(obviously Twain) kills his conscience. Twain complained repeatedly and
vociferously in his private writings about being hounded by his "yellow-
dog of a conscience." Numerous times he suffered anguish and remorse
because his Presbyterian conscience saddled him with undeserved guilt.
To cite only the major instances: he blamed himself needlessly for the
deaths of his brother Henry (in a steamboat accident), his only son
Langdon (from pneumonia), and his beloved daughter Susy (from spinal
meningitis). In the 1890's he embraced environmental determinism, a
philosophy which enabled him to shed at last his burden of imagined
guilt. If, indeed, all events in the universe were predetermined and attribut-
able to forces beyond the control of a single human being, he need not
feel at fault. Thus Twain finally vanquished his conscience, but he failed
to enjoy the "unalloyed bliss" depicted in the story two decades earlier.
The relief came too late.

"The Carnival of Crime" does not appear in Charles Neider's collection, perhaps because he considered it too autobiographical. The story is readily available, though, in the Reiss edition of *The Mysterious Stranger and Other Stories.*

MAXWELL GEISMAR
A CURIOUS PARABLE
"The Recent Carnival of Crime"

Reprinted in Twain's collected works as "The Facts Concerning the Recent Carnival of Crime in Connecticut," this story was actually the prelude to a dark line of surrealistic parables which would include *Pudd'nhead Wilson,* "The Man That Corrupted Hadleyburg," and *The Mysterious Stranger,* in a different and more complex vein of Clemens' talent. Here we meet "the shriveled, shabby dwarf" who is about forty years old and no more than two feet high—this little person who is a deformity as a whole, "a vague, general, evenly blended, nicely adjusted deformity." And yet, "this vile bit of human rubbish seemed to bear a sort of remote and ill-defined resemblance to me!" He knows everything that goes on in the narrator's (Clemens') mind and spirit; he knows all his lies, vices, and sins, his arrogance, dishonesty, faithlessness, disloyalty, fits of violent anger, remorse. Clemens paints a very low view of himself here, and it is recognizable, until the narrator suddenly accuses his tormentor of being the devil, of being Satan himself. In this dubious shifting light, Clemens stresses his life-long affinity with the fallen angel. But the odious and moldy dwarf turns out to be not the devil or Satan at all, but Twain's *conscience.*

And while the autobiographical narrator of the story is being roundly abused by his Conscience, he in turn abuses his Conscience and is intent upon capturing and killing the malignant dwarf. "Dwarf," as the dwarf explains, because while originally he started out precisely as tall as Clemens, his being neglected and abused through the years has steadily reduced his stature and power.

From *Mark Twain: An American Prophet* by Maxwell Geismar. Copyright © 1970 by Maxwell Geismar. Used by permission of the publisher, Houghton Mifflin Company (title is editor's).

What abuse and self-abuse abounds in this curious parable; what violence of language in Clemens' charges and counter-charges. "My good slave, you are curiously witless—no, I mean characteristically so. In truth, you are always consistent, always yourself, always an ass," says Clemens' Conscience to Clemens, addressing him in his own "s-n-i-v-e-l-l-i-n-g d-r-a-w-l —baby!" while the outraged victim of this impudence is plotting the sudden demise of the insolent demon. "If I only had you shrunk down to a homeopathic pill, and could get my hands on you, would I put you in a glass case for a keepsake? No, sir. I would give you to a yellow dog! That is where *you* ought to be . . ." Now was the "aunt" of this story— always reproaching the Clemens narrator for his smoking, among other vices, rather like the Aunt Polly of *Tom Sawyer*—a mother surrogate or a wife surrogate? It is her intrusion, at any rate, which allows the dualistic and divided hero to achieve his deadly purpose. "My breath was coming in short, quick gasps now, and my excitement was almost uncontrollable. My aunt cried out: 'Oh, do not look so! You appal me! Oh, what can the matter be? What is it you see? Why do you stare so? Why do you work your fingers like that?' " While the aunt pleads hysterically with the hero to drop the vices which lead to such fits, Clemens' Conscience "began to reel drowsily and grope with his hands—enchanting spectacle!" and droops languidly to the floor "blinking toward me a last supplication for mercy, with heavy eyes," when

With an exultant shout I sprang past my aunt, and in an instant I had my lifelong foe by the throat. After so many years of waiting and longing, he was mine at last. I tore him to shreds and fragments. I rent the fragments into bits. I cast the bleeding rubbish into the fire, and drew into my nostrils the grateful incense of my burnt-offering. At last, and forever, my Conscience was dead!

This was the history of the narrator's "freedom" in "The Recent Carnival of Crime," as his aunt, with all her charities and mercies, flies from him in terror; and in "bliss, unalloyed bliss" he embarks upon a criminal career.

Now in orthodox Freudian terms this story is just what it sounds like, and orthodox Freudians can shake their heads sadly and commiserate ad nauseam over poor Sam Clemens' burden of sin and guilt. In Rankian cultural terms, however, what this story marks (as Clemens must have felt and known in his depths) is the hero's *liberation* from the repressive burden of civilizational discontents, his defiance of conventional morality, his determination to be himself at all costs (every artist's design)—and hence, the "bliss, unalloyed bliss," of Clemens' natural spirit, and the carnival of crime which is the organism's realization it is enjoying itself despite the dictates of society. —A kind of vestigial guilt, yes, which is laughing at itself. This curious parable, so much harped upon by conventional depth psychology, proves to be the exact opposite, or the true rationale of art and the artist. This was Sam Clemens exorcising his Puritan past.

And why not? Clemens was riding high in those days. And yet the mixed tone of the fable, and the curious confusion of Satan, who is the obvious symbol of pagan life, with his own conscience, rather than, as elsewhere, with his true temperament, indicated certain strains in Eden.

WILLIAM M. GIBSON
MARK TWAIN'S "CARNIVAL OF CRIME"

The role of "the moral sense" in Mark Twain's "The Chronicle of Young Satan" and other late works is vividly foreshadowed in a remarkable story with an almost opaque title, "The Facts Concerning the Recent Carnival of Crime in Connecticut." This fanciful narrative, which appeared early in 1876, is so intensely dramatic that it might be adapted to the stage without difficulty. It is also an allegory of the human psyche—foreshadowing Freud and depth psychology, and an astonishing bit of Clemens's autobiography spoken through the mask of Mark Twain.

The "Carnival of Crime" is told, first-person colloquial, in Mark Twain's best confidential—even confessional—manner. It gives every appearance of being no more than a "humorous story" floating along in a leisurely way, open to elaboration. It involves in fact a tightly wrought confrontation between the storyteller and his conscience, full of growing anguish and suspense, in which the narrator's loved and honored Aunt Mary plays a vital (if small) role. The story opens with Mark Twain feeling "blithe, almost jocund" as he lights his cigar and learns with great satisfaction from the morning mail that his Aunt Mary is to visit him and will in fact be arriving soon. She could still stir his "torpid conscience" in the matter of his "pernicious habit" of smoking—but only faintly. So strong is his euphoria that he feels he might now make peace with his "most pitiless enemy."

From *The Art of Mark Twain* (New York: Oxford University Press, 1976), pp. 178-184. Reprinted by permission.

At this very moment the door opens, admitting a two-foot-tall dwarf who bears a caricature resemblance to the narrator and is covered with a "fuzzy greenish mould." The manikin insolently demands a match, lights one of Mark Twain's pipes, and in a mocking drawl remarks that it's "devilish odd weather." The pigmy with the weasel eyes ignores his host's resentment and opens attack upon him, with increasingly alarming inside knowledge of misdeeds which "Mark Twain" has been ashamed of. That very morning he had turned a hungry tramp from the door with a lie, and the other day he had refused to read a young woman's manuscript and made her weep—so the "small fiend" reminds him. He had punished his children unjustly, and had "disloyally allowed old friends to be traduced" in his hearing—so the dwarf persists, taking obvious pleasure in the narrator's increasing remorse. Worse still, Mark Twain is reminded of his tricking his younger brother into an ice-filled brook when they were boys together; and worst of all, there was that "peculiarly mean and pitiful act . . . toward a poor ignorant Indian . . . in the winter of eighteen hundred and—," a memory so painful that he cannot permit the dwarf to go on with his recital. The accusations grow stronger and move back in time into the narrator's youth and childhood. Challenged as Satan—the Devil himself—the dwarf reveals to Mark Twain that he is his *Conscience*.

In a murderous rage the narrator fires the poker, books, inkstands, and chunks of coal at his tormentor, but Conscience, "light as a feather," darts to the top of a high bookcase and laughs at his "slave." Locking the door and declaring a truce for the moment, he begins to catechize Conscience, rather in the spirit of Dr. Faustus querying Mephistopheles, and learns that Conscience is usually invisible and insubstantial, but still quite moral. More, Conscience, that "ashcat," is neither his friend nor his equal: he is enemy and master—and takes the profoundest satisfaction in punishing his slave, pegging at him night and day, year in and year out, never letting his subject off for any offense. While the effect may be to improve a man, the intent of Conscience is to punish. He and other Consciences take special pleasure, for example, in hazing people of a "peculiarly sensitive nature," and it is his *business* to make the author suffer, whether he feeds a tramp and encourages vagrancy or refuses food to the tramp and feels mean, to repent of *everything* he does.

The debate turns to the size of consciences, and Conscience reveals that he was seven feet tall and "pretty as a picture" when Mark Twain was a boy, but has since shriveled and grown mouldy and lethargic. Mark Twain wants to know about his neighbor Thompson's conscience. Once eleven feet tall and of faultless figure (Conscience replies), he is now rusty and dull—and "sleeps in a cigar box." Robinson's? Robinson's conscience is four and one-half feet tall, shapely and comely still. Tom Smith's? When

Smith was two years old, his conscience was thirteen inches tall and sluggish—like others in babyhood; now, however, he is thirty-seven feet tall and still growing, and never sleeps. Smith is president of the New England Conscience Club and is always heartbroken "because he cannot be good!" His Aunt Mary's? Her conscience lives out-of-doors entirely, for no door is big enough to admit her. And what of the publisher who once stole some Mark Twain sketches for a "series," and made him pay the law expenses to "choke him off"? At a recent exhibit of consciences (Conscience replies) the publisher's conscience was to have been the main feature—but no one could see it, since the management's microscope magnified only to thirty thousand diameters.

When Aunt Mary arrives, and in her mild, good-hearted way is soon reproaching her nephew for neglecting a poor family in the neighborhood, Conscience droops heavily on his bookcase perch. She reminds him how he has neglected her protégée at the almshouse—and Conscience falls to the floor, squirming feebly. Only when Aunt Mary supplicates her nephew to give up "this hateful slavery of tobacco" does Conscience reel drowsily and fall fast asleep. With an exultant shout, Mark Twain seizes Conscience by the throat, tears him to bloody fragments, and burns the fragments in the fire. Conscience is dead, and he is a free man.

In a change like that of Dr. Jekyll into Mr. Hyde—except for the narrator's comic exaggeration and the sympathy the reader still must feel for him—"Mark Twain," a "man WITHOUT A CONSCIENCE," rejects his Aunt Mary's paupers and reform and pestilential morals, and ejects her from the house. His life since that day is unalloyed bliss, he tells us. He kills thirty-eight people whom he has old grudges against; burns down a building that spoils his view; swindles a widow and orphans of their last cow, and enters on a carnival of crime. The anticlimactic order of these crimes prevents the reader from taking "Mark Twain" the narrator of this story as a Raskolnikov, and the business jargon and flat prose of the last paragraph set firmly the key of burlesque:

In conclusion I wish to state, by way of advertisement, that medical colleges desiring assorted tramps for scientific purposes, either by the gross, by cord measurement, or per ton, will do well to examine the lot in my cellar before purchasing elsewhere, as these were all selected and prepared by myself, and can be had at a low rate, because I wish to clear out my stock and get ready for the spring trade.

The tone is burlesque, but the author still manages his point: his *persona,* free of conscience, has murdered those who annoy him, and will murder more who do so in the future.

The autobiographical element in the "Carnival of Crime" is fairly strong. Although Aunt Mary is fictional and typical, like Aunt Polly in *Tom Sawyer* (which was scheduled for publication a few months later), the portrait owes several traits to Olivia Clemens, especially her early aversion to her husband's smoking. The allusion to the larcenous publisher would be clear enough to Mark Twain's friends, for W. F. Gill had included "An Encounter with an Interviewer" in the first volume of *The Treasure Trove Series,* and used the Mark Twain *nom de plume* without permission. Gill's conscience, one notes, is so small as to be all but invisible. The "budding authoress" certainly seems real. She may be composite. But the contemptuous and mocking reference by Conscience to "your o-w-n s-n-i-v-e-l-l-i-n-g d-r-a-w-l—baby!" is a direct and personal reference to Clemens's "drawling infirmity of speech." Howells queried the phrase; his friend asked whether it seemed too personal; the speech remained unaltered.

One wonders, too, whether the unidentified trick played on an Indian—perhaps a Goshoot, of a tribe he detested—was based on a deed he had perpetrated or was a creation of Mark Twain's imagination. Similarly, while young Sam Clemens may not have pushed a trusting younger brother blindfolded into an icy brook, the episode figures in "No. 44, The Mysterious Stranger" and in "Villagers of 1840-3," and Clemens *did* play practical jokes on his younger brother Henry. Above all, self-blame and Conscience's "hazing" of a man of "peculiarly sensitive nature," and the rebellion against a rarely-still conscience are recognizable facts of the history of Clemens's inner life. The "Carnival of Crime" makes unusually frank—and effective—use of the author's own experience.

The Freudian dimension of the tale might be defined fully by a practicing Freudian critic, which I am not. Nonetheless, anyone with an elementary awareness of psychoanalytical concepts can see that Mark Twain anticipated Freud (who, we know, read the humorist with pleasure) in several striking ways, particularly in his chapter "The Anatomy of the Mental Personality" in *New Introductory Lectures on Psycho-Analysis.* In his description of "the anatomy of the mental personality," for example, Freud occasionally uses effective metaphors, such as a cracked crystal for the complex relations of Germans, Magyars, and Slovaks, and the sustained metaphors of geography, exploration, and the "anatomy" of the psyche. Most vividly, he personifies superego, id, and external world as "harsh masters," and creates a genuine drama in which the ego, crying "Life is not easy," must make a go of life by reconciling the divergent and even incompatible demands of its three masters.

Freud begins with the astonishing fact that the ego can take itself as an object of study or observation, criticize itself, and "do Heaven knows what besides with itself." It can even, in the case of Mark Twain, write a profound and very funny "metaphysical" narrative arising from the power of conscience, the conscious portion of the superego, to observe, criticize, and sustain ideals. Thus, in the "Carnival of Crime," the narrator plays the role of the tormented ego, his Aunt Mary represents parents and other authority figures as a "vehicle of tradition" in training the superego, the mouldy dwarf is the narrator's conscience or conscious part of the superego, and the id approximately remains invisible in the unconscious, but quite evident in the compulsively demonic behavior of the narrator-ego at the end of the "Carnival." Freud observes that the superego abuses and humiliates the ego and threatens it with severest punishment, just as (conscious) Conscience torments Mark Twain's narrator, especially for "long-forgotten actions" such as his ill-treatment of his brother or the bad turn done to the Indian in the Rocky Mountain West. Freud theorizes that conscience works intermittently, and may be heavy or light in different people: "A great many men have only a limited share of it or scarcely enough to be worth mentioning."

Mark Twain prefigures the proposition in the change of his conscience from seven feet tall and attractive to dwarfish and disgusting; and in the varying sizes and weights of those of Thompson, Robinson, Smith, Aunt Mary, and the publisher. Even the remark that "small children are notoriously amoral" is prefigured in the statement that Robinson's conscience, now thirty-seven feet tall, had been thirteen inches tall "and rather sluggish, when he was two years old—as nearly all of us are, at that age," and shares Freud's view that the superego is acquired, not innately present, like sexuality.

And so the drama is played out: Mark Twain as ego destroys his master or lord, Conscience, terrifies and banishes his Aunt Mary, and enters upon a joyful "carnival of crime." Freud concluded his essay with the famous dictum, "Where id was, there shall ego be." Mark Twain dramatizes the reverse idea, "Where superego was, there shall id be." Bernard Shaw attributed to Mark Twain a piece of wisdom to the effect that "telling the truth's the funniest joke in the world." This is the distinction of "Carnival of Crime," and the product of Mark Twain's high art and thorough craftsmanship.

5

THE £1,000,000 BANK-NOTE

Although "The £1,000,000 Bank-Note" was written in 1892 and first printed in January of 1893 in *Century Magazine,* the plot was outlined during happier times in June 1883. The singular optimism of the story perhaps stems in part from this early planning, but more likely Twain intended to satirize the mindless confidence of the American dream in which money equals success equals happiness. The story reflects a number of Horatio Alger elements: a clean-living, (formerly) hard-working hero, a beautiful maiden receptive to his charms, a magical and meteoric rise to millions, and a society in which a man is judged not by the strength of his character but by the size of his bank account. It was Twain, after all, who named this period of burgeoning materialism "The Gilded Age." In his private papers he recalled wistfully the finer days of his youth:

All that sentimentality and romance among young folks seem puerile, now, but when one examines it and compares it with the ideals of today, it was a preferable thing. It was soft, sappy, melancholy; but money had no place in it. To get rich was no one's ambition—it was not in any young person's thoughts. . . . It was an intensely sentimental age, but it took no sordid form.

By the time Twain wrote this story, he was already suffering serious financial difficulties. For years he had been pouring money into the development of an intricate typesetting machine, which promised millions in profits but instead lost him a total of $190,000. His household expenses at the Hartford mansion continued to soar. And the publishing company he had established in order to increase his royalties was instead beginning to diminish his fortune. In 1891 he once more moved his family to Europe in an attempt to economize on living expenses and to benefit, if possible, his wife's faltering health.

With these grave financial troubles weighing on him, Twain could scarcely have written this story dramatizing the American dream of success as anything but satire. For him the dream was already becoming a nightmare.

PHILIP S. FONER
A SATIRE ON THE SYSTEM

Twain's celebrated short story, "The Million Pound Bank Note," recently made into a delightful film by the British moviemaker Ronald Neame, presents his acid comments on a society that treats people according to how much money they have. The tale revolves about a bet between two immensely rich old Londoners over whether the simple possession of a million pound note would be enough to insure the future of the man who held it, even if he never cashed it. To resolve the argument they turn the bill over to an impoverished American passer-by, with the instructions to return it in a month's time and claim his reward. At once a despised tramp is changed into the object of respect and veneration. And the irony of it all is that it is the appearance of money and not the money itself that really counts. As long as the American has his scrap of paper, his credit is unlimited. The finest restaurants, tailors, and hotels—even the finest homes—are open to him. An occasional flash of the note is sufficient to establish his credit. He can make stocks rise at the mere mention of his interest in them. And, of course, he promptly becomes England's most eligible bachelor.

Twain's farcical story brilliantly satirizes a system based not so much on money as the appearance of money. Again Twain makes the point that it is not character but possession of wealth that determines a man's standing in his contemporary society. The possession of great wealth did not give the American in the story real happiness. Yet, Twain points out,

---

From *Mark Twain: Social Critic* (New York: International Publishers, 1958), pp. 160–161. Reprinted by permission of the publisher (title is editor's).

people threw away their whole lives for it, only to discover that its pleasures were feverish and transient. As he put it in the closing paragraph of the story "The $30,000 Bequest," in which this theme is developed: "Vast wealth, acquired by sudden and unwholesome means, is a snare."

MAXWELL GEISMAR
MARK TWAIN ON THE "GET-RICH-QUICK" MANIA

"The £1,000,000 Bank-Note," published in 1893 and inserted in a later edition of *Merry Tales,* was a trick tale of a young American who was given a fabulous sum of money as part of a betting proposition between two British financiers. It is another ironic parable of unexpected (and undeserved) wealth; and it is interesting to notice how many other stories by Mark Twain in the early nineties dealt with various aspects of this theme. The get-rich-quick mania was the central folk myth of the period; and wasn't Samuel Clemens himself an example of his historical American dream—or nightmare? This was the period of boom and depression in steady succession; of financial wizardry and fiscal legerdemain; of the great Wall Street battles for control, power and manipulation of the new corporations, combines, and monopolies. It was the period of our "interior colonization," so to speak—the development of the internal American empire which, having devoured the enormous wealth of one continent, would soon stretch out its claws for tempting foreign treats. The dominance of this new tribe of cunning, ruthless, unscrupulous, and amoral financial titans and tycoons would change the whole nature of American life as Sam Clemens had known it. In another sense his work may be interpreted as half a lyrical recall of the past, and half an angry, bitter, savage attack on contemporary American society and what he called the future "monarchy" or dictatorship.

RICKI MORGAN

MARK TWAIN'S MONEY IMAGERY IN
"THE £1,000,000 BANK-NOTE" AND
"THE $30,000 BEQUEST"

Samuel Clemens, in an attempt to achieve vast returns quickly, invested in all sorts of inventions which brought him to financial ruin. In the ten year period (1893-1903) after he fell into indebtedness, he wrote to earn money to extricate himself from his creditors. It does not appear surprising that the central concern of two of the stories he wrote during that time is the sudden acquisition of vast sums of money which turn out to be chimerical or unspendable. "The £1,000,000 Bank-Note" (1893) is about a pauper suddenly given a bank-note for that amount which cannot be cashed, and "The $30,000 Bequest" (1903) is about an inheritance which never existed. Yet the endings of the stories are diametrically opposed to each other. In "Bank-Note," the ending is that of a fairy-tale romance. In "Bequest," it is total annihilation and death. Are these differences due to a thematic inconsistency or changing philosophy on Twain's part? I hope to show they are not.

In both stories it appears that money is depicted as "The great tempter." After the fall from Eden, Adam's curse was his necessity to work by the sweat of his brow. For Mark Twain, I feel, to try to circumvent this, and come into large fortunes of "easy money," is to try to defy man's fate, and is an enterprise doomed to failure. The man who engages in such enterprises is guilty of the sin of avarice. If man is morally weak, and values money more than his soul, he is guilty of a moral failing for which, in Twain's works, it appears that he will fall greviously. However, if the temptation of "easy money" is successfully withstood, if man has the moral fiber to value true wealth of character over monetary gains, it is then, I believe, that Twain's providence rewards him.

"£1,000,000 Bank-Note" appears to be a story of temptation successfully withstood and ultimately rewarded. "$30,000 Bequest," on the other hand deals with a couple who worship money instead of God, fall sorely, and are completely destroyed by their greed.

There is strong evidence that the £1,000,000 bank-note is meant to offer a powerful temptation to a ruinous fate. It is furnished by two men who coldly gamble on whether or not Henry Adams will manage to last

From *Mark Twain Journal,* 19 (Winter 1977-78), 6-10. Used by permission of Cyril Clemens, editor of the *Mark Twain Journal.*

a month with it. The temptation of money as "original sin," the root of all evil, is hinted at in Twain's naming the protagonist Adams. An association with the original Adam is brought to mind in the dispute over the oldest peerage that Adams has with the Duke of Shoreditch:

It couldn't be settled, of course, struggle as we might and did, he finally (and injudiciously) trying to play birth and antiquity, and I "seeing" his Conqueror and "raising" him with Adam, whose direct posterity I was, as shown by my name, while *he* was of a collateral branch, as shown by *his,* and by his recent Norman origin (p. 327).

The linking of money with the fall of man seems to be further hinted at in the imagery which surrounds Adams' receipt of the bank-note. He stands hungrily in front of the house of his future "benefactors" watching a piece of fruit; "a luscious big pear—*minus one bite*" (p. 316), which is tolled before him. It would be too shameful for him to be seen picking up the fruit and eating it, but "I was just getting desperate enough to brave all the shame, and to seize it, when a window behind me was raised, and a gentleman spoke out of it, saying:
'Step in here please'" (p. 317).

Once he has received the envelope with the bank-note, and returns out into the street, Adam says, "I would have picked up the pear now and eaten it before all the world, but it was gone" (p. 318). Adams receives the bank-note when he is about to eat the forbidden fruit, and after he has accepted it, the fruit is gone.

In the beginning of the story we are told that this descendant of Adam is ideally equipped to withstand the temptation of "easy money" and is prepared to work hard and honestly for a living:

When I was twenty-seven years old, I was a mining-broker's clerk in San Francisco, and an expert in all the details of stock traffic. I was alone in the world, and had nothing to depend upon but my wits and a clean reputation; but these were setting my feet in the road to eventual fortune, and I was content with the prospect (p. 316).

We learn that he has withstood such temptation in the past. At the dinner party, his former employer recalls how a few months ago

I tried to persuade you to come to London with me, and offered to get leave of absence for you and pay all your expenses, and give you something over if I succeeded in making the sale; and you would not listen to me, said I wouldn't succeed, and you couldn't afford to lose the run of business and be no end of time getting the hang of things again when you got back home (p. 326).

Adams' bank-note begins propelling him into his startling position of prominence not through his own greed and money worship, but through the greed and money worship of the society surrounding him. Thinking he was given a gift of a pound note, he goes into "the nearest cheap eating house" and eats his fill. Adams takes out the note to pay his bill and discovers its denomination. After getting over his initial shock, "the first thing I noticed was the landlord. His eye was on the note. . . . He was worshipping, with all his body and soul" (p. 318). Adams does the only "rational thing to do," and offers the note in payment, asking for change. The proprietor "Wanted to look at it and keep on looking at it; he couldn't seem to get enough of it to quench the thirst of his eye, but he shrank from touching it as if it had been something too sacred to handle" (p. 318). It is this worship of money by the people who surround Adams, and not any dishonesty on Adams' part, that propels him to prominence. Adams is frank about his situation, but the landlord is overwhelmed by the sight of the bill and pays him no heed. Adams asks for change, telling him he hasn't anything else,

But he said that wasn't any matter; he was quite willing to let the trifle stand over till another time. I said I might not be in his neighborhood again for a good while; but he said it was of no consequence, he could wait, and, moreover, I could have anything I wanted, any time I chose, and let the account run as long as I pleased (p. 319).

Adams' first real temptation is the extended credit on a million pounds that doesn't belong to him. But at this point he pays it no heed and runs off to act with honesty, to return the note to its proprietors. He regards the note as "the monster," rather than an object of reverential worship, and goes off to return it post haste.

After Adams discovers that he is being made a loan "for thirty days without interest" and will receive any situation that he is able to prove himself "familiar with and competent to fill" (p. 320), he is not tempted to get credit against the loan. What leads him into temptation is the confidence that he can prove himself capable of deserving a good position and earning his bread by his work: "I got to thinking a good deal about that situation. My hopes began to rise high. Without doubt the salary would be large. It would begin in a month; after that I should be all right" (p. 321). He then passes a tailor shop, and is seized by

a sharp longing to shed my rags, and to clothe myself decently once more . . . . The temptation persecuted me cruelly. I must have passed that shop back and forth six times during that manful struggle. At last I gave in; I had to (p. 321).

But even his temptation is of the most modest kind; he only banks on being able to afford "a misfit suit."

He goes into the store, asks for the misfit suit and is treated with commensurate disdain. After being kept waiting, the salesman, "took me into a back room, and overhauled a pile of rejected suits, and selected the rattiest one for me" (p. 321). Once again, Adams' bank-note shows up the money worshipping values of the others around him. He asks for the suit on credit, is treated with contempt. As soon as he mentions he can pay for the suit but didn't want to put the salesman to the trouble of changing a large bill, the salesman "modified his style a little at that." After the appearance of the bank-note, the proprietor comes in, and the treatment given Adams is completely reversed:

Please get those things off, sir, and throw them in the fire. Do me the favor to put on this shirt and this suit; . . . made to order for a foreign prince—you may know him, sir, his Serene Highness the Hospodar of Halifax (p. 322).

Once again, Adams is honest about his inability to pay, but the sight of the bank-note makes the proprietor again disregard him. The credit he was previously denied is extended to him "indefinitely."

Adams accepts the loan, but is filled with trepidation:

I judged there was going to be a crash by and by. . . . You see there was just the element of impending disaster to give a serious, a sober side, yes, a tragic side to this state of things which would otherwise have been purely ridiculous (p. 323).

Adams' bank-note makes him a celebrity. In the gossip columns of the newspaper, "I reached the highest altitude possible . . . taking precedence over all dukes not royal" (p. 324). However, although he takes loans and credit, he is careful not to incur any debts which he won't be able to work off. He takes nothing which he does not contemplate paying back:

At present I was only in debt for my first year's salary. Everybody had been trying to lend me money, but I had fought off the most of them on one pretext or another; so this indebtedness represented only £300 borrowed money, the other £300 represented by keep and purchases (p. 325).

Adams' nature is perhaps most clearly displayed in, and reaps its greatest reward for, his wooing of Portia Langdon. Like Shakespeare's Portia, the way to win this girl is by choosing the "lead casket"; realizing that true wealth resides in her person. Adams immediately makes a clean breast to her of his true financial straights. He never inquires into her fortune or family, and tells her she will have to expect to live in poverty for a while, and it will be a couple of years before they can get married. When Portia laughs after hearing the story of his adversity, Adams finds that

I loved her all the more, seeing she could be so cheerful when there wasn't anything to be cheerful about; for I might soon need that kind of wife, you know, the way things looked (p. 328).

Adams is rewarded for his uprightness but we see God helping those who help themselves. He earns his money not from any gift given him, but by using his intellect—honestly, and generously. He devises a scheme to help his friend Hastings (whose predicament is a result of his attempt to make "easy money" with his mining stock deal). When Hastings asks Adams to help him by buying the stock,

a white-hot idea came flaming through my head, and I gripped my jaws together, and calmed myself down till I was as cold as a capitalist. Then I said, in a commercial and self-possessed way,
"I will save you Lloyd . . . I know all about that mine, of course; I know its immense value, and can swear to it if anybody wishes it. You shall sell out inside of the fortnight for three millions cash, using my name freely, and we'll divide, share and share alike" (p. 331).

So Adams gets wealth by his own efforts, and not through any gifts bolting out of the blue. This is made clear at the end of the story where it is also indicated that although he has money, this is not where he considers his true wealth to lie:

My Portia's papa took that friendly and hospitable bill back to the Bank of England and cashed it; then the Bank canceled it . . . and he gave it to us at our wedding, and it has always hung in its frame in the sacredest place in our home ever since. For it gave me my Portia. . . . And so I always say, "Yes, it's a million pounder, as you see; but it never made but one purchase in its life, and *then* got the article for only about a tenth part of its value" (p. 334).

So huge sums of unspendable money can make vast purchases, but only when its receiver is aware of where true wealth lies.

In "Bank-Note" Adams was given a vast sum of real but unspendable money; his strong moral fiber kept him from real ruination and gave him a concrete reward. In "Bequest" the situation is curiously reversed. The Fosters are given a vast sum of imaginary money which they are free to imaginarily spend and invest. Their real life and real situation are not changed. The only thing in jeopardy is their imaginary life, their souls. So powerful is the force of greed, so dangerous is the placing of material wealth over spiritual wealth, that the loss of money they never possessed, and the return to a life that they never left, destroys them.

One of the most prominent themes in this story, and one that seems central to the story's meaning, is the religious attitudes of the Fosters. Mr. Foster's nature appears to be greedy and impious, a dangerous personality in Twain's universe. Electra, his wife's outlook appears more dangerous still. She has a cash-nexus view of God and of religion. She is unable to distinguish between spiritual "investments" and monetary ones. While Saladin Foster is capable of recognizing his irreverence and greed, even though he chooses not to reform, Mrs. Foster is incapable of even seeing her sins, of telling right from wrong. Consequently, any sort of repentance or reformation is even beyond her imagining. As Saladin says to her, when discussing her piety,

I didn't mean so bad as that Aleck; I didn't really mean immoral piety. I only meant—meant—well, conventional piety, you know; er—shop piety; the—the why, you know what I mean, Aleck—the—well, where you put up the plated article and play it for solid, you know, without intending anything improper, but just out of trade habit, ancient policy, petrified custom, loyalty to—to—hang it, I can't find the right words but *you* know what I mean. . . . (p. 506).

The ironic part is that Mrs. Foster, by her self-righteous indignation during these frequent religious discussions with her husband, indicates that she does not know. She has been "playing the plated article for genuine" for so long that she has convinced herself of its solidity. Unfortunately, her husband will never convince her to the contrary. As their nicknames indicate, (Saladin's is Sally, and Electra's is Aleck) she is the dominant figure, her mercantile morality governs. Any such conversation with her husband always ends with his apologizing to her.

The "money" is left to the Fosters with their dying uncle's curse. The only provision for the inheritance is that the Fosters act totally ungrateful,

that Sally should be able to prove to the executors that he had *taken no notice of the gift by spoken word or by letter, had made no inquiries concerning the moribund's progress toward the everlasting tropics, and had not attended the funeral* (p. 502).

If there were true Christian sentiment among the couple, the money, of course, would pose no more threat to them than the possession of the bank-note did for Adams. They would immediately have done what was honorable, and their duty. They would have gone to Uncle Tilbury's death-bed and asked for his dying blessing, instead of his curse. But their behavior is quite the opposite:

> Man and wife entered into a solemn compact, now, to never mention the great news to anyone while the relative lived, lest some ignorant person carry the fact to the death-bed and distort it and make it appear that they were disobediently thankful for the bequest, and just the same as confessing it and publishing it, right in the face of the prohibition (p. 502).

If the disposal of the "wealth" were left in the hands of Sally's simple greed, it would pose little threat to the Fosters' well being; he would have squandered it on imaginary purchases the first evening. The bubble would have burst at the outset, leaving no more than a passing pang of disappointment. But Aleck's acquisitive greed extends far beyond her husband's. She must invest the imaginary windfall into a vast imaginary fortune before she will allow Sally to "touch a penny" of the wealth.

After five weeks, Sally's simple greed is conquered by natural curiosity. Were he able to assert himself now, the situation would have ceased after five weeks instead of five years. But Aleck's cold, cautious acquisitiveness will not let this happen:

> Sally now resolved to brace up and risk a frontal attack. So he squarely proposed to disguise himself and go to Tilbury's village and surreptitiously find out as to the prospects. Aleck put her foot on the dangerous project with energy and decision (p. 508).

Due to Aleck's "speculations" the imaginary wealth increases to a vast sum. They are completely overwhelmed by their greed which grows in like proportion. First they "fell—and broke the sabbath" to count their imaginary money. Then Sally starts stealing candles from the shop he works in so they can stay up at night figuring their investments. Aleck's greed even corrupts her imaginary investments. She has "holdings" in "Tammany Graft and Shady Privileges in the Post-office Department" (p. 515). From this point on, Twain punctuates his story with homilies like the following: "Vast wealth has temptations which fatally and surely undermine the moral structure of persons not habituated to its possession" (p. 515). I feel such interspersions most likely are meant to be interpreted as ironic, since the Fosters aren't corrupted by "vast wealth"—they do not have a penny more than they did at the beginning of the story; rather, it appears that their corrupt natures in the form of snowballing greed has brought them to their present state.

Aleck has lost herself in their greed to the point where, when she loses her imaginary money in an imaginary investment, her despair and ruination are quite real. Sally has almost, but not quite, reached her stage. He has the presence of mind to realize that the money lost is imaginary. However, it is this last accurate observation that rekindles the spark of greed back to its height, so that they are totally annihilated when they learn that the bequest is nonexistent:

You really never invested a penny of my uncle's bequest, but only its unmaterialized future; what we have lost was only the increment harvested from that future. . . . Cheer up. . . , we still have the thirty thousand untouched; and with the experience which you have acquired, think what you will be able to do with it in a couple of years! (p. 523).

Once they find out that there will never be any money forthcoming their *raison d'être* is gone, and they succumb to death. If they had learned where true spiritual wealth lies, they could never have been robbed of existence by the chimerical kind. On Sally's death-bed, he appears to come to a partial realization of the truth:

Vast wealth acquired by sudden and unwholesome means is a snare. It did us no good, transient were its feverish pleasures; yet for its sake we threw away our sweet and simple and happy life—let others take warning by us (p. 525).

But Sally's spiritual insight is as weak and as fluctuating as his imaginary fortune. Instead of repenting his moral frailty with his dying breath, and resolving that if he had his life to live over he would place spiritual wealth over temporal, he curses his uncle for not leaving them a larger imaginary fortune, so that they wouldn't have been tempted to lose it in an imaginary speculation.

It appears that "vast wealth acquired by sudden and unwholesome means" is a snare and brings ruination. However, ruination is not brought about by the "vast wealth" itself, but by the "sudden and unwholesome means" of acquisition. Vast wealth alone poses no threat to the uncorruptable Adams, but the "sudden and unwholesome means" without real wealth is sufficient to destroy the morally deficient Fosters.

6

THE MAN THAT CORRUPTED
HADLEYBURG

The bitter tale about Hadleyburg was written near the end of a decade during which Twain's financial difficulties matured into disasters. At the beginning of the 1890's that "cunning devil," the typesetting machine, was consuming four thousand dollars a month—money, Albert Bigelow Paine testifies, that constituted "the final gleanings and sweepings of every nook and corner of the strong-box and bank-account and savings of the Clemens family resources." A few years later the Paige typesetter was rendered obsolete by the marketing of the superior Mergenthaler linotype. The fortune lost on the machine "would better have been thrown into the Connecticut River," says Paine, "for then the agony had been more quickly over" (p. 912).

Twain's publishing company during this same period was undergoing a severe fiscal crisis. In April of 1894 he was forced to declare bankruptcy. Nearing sixty and close to $100,000 in debt, he resolved to pay back one hundred cents on the dollar, although the law required only half this amount. "Honor," he declared, "is a harder master than the law." In 1895 he set off on a strenuous lecture tour of the English-speaking world in order to reimburse his creditors.

His favorite daughter Susy, then twenty-four years old, dreaded ocean travel and chose to remain in Elmira with her aunt. Exactly a year and a day after his departure, on August 15, 1896, he was standing in the dining room of his London lodgings, "thinking of nothing in particular," when he received a cablegram reading, "Susy was peacefully released today." Her death was perhaps the greatest tragedy of his life. "It is one of the mysteries of our nature," he later wrote, "that a man, all unprepared, can receive a thunder-stroke like that and live" (quoted by Justin Kaplan).

In 1897 the family moved to Vienna for the winter so that the eldest daughter, Clara, could study the piano under Leschetizky. Here in 1898 Twain wrote "The Man That Corrupted Hadleyburg," which appeared in *Harper's* in December of 1899. This ironic story, which is a resounding tirade against the hypocrisy of "the damned human race," reflects Twain's deepening pessimism after the trials of a disastrous decade.

GLADYS BELLAMY
MORALISM VERSUS DETERMINISM IN "HADLEYBURG"

The mind of Mark Twain was a workshop in which two creatures were constantly busy, a creature of hope and a creature of despair. Despite their enforced intimacy, they were not on good terms; their natures were far too different. Sometimes one would cow the other into temporary submission so that he could finish a piece of work—hurriedly, perhaps; but often one—that is, whichever began first—would be challenged by the other, who would insist on doing a part of the job his way. There were always two Mark Twains, the Moralist *versus* the Determinist. Let us see what these two workmen made of *The Man That Corrupted Hadleyburg,* praised by Paine as his greatest short story, "wonderfully done": "The mechanism of the story is perfect, the drama of it is . . . supreme in its artistic triumph." It deals with the force of environment, since "temptations were kept out of the way of the young people, so that their honesty could have every chance to harden and solidify." But in another passage this environmental training is shown as powerless to change underlying human nature: ". . . it's been one ever-lasting training and training and training in honesty—honesty shielded, from the cradle, against every possible temptation, and so it's *artificial* honesty, and weak as water when temptation comes. . . ." There is deterministic motivation through the force of circumstances in the guise of "the stranger." Almost half a hundred citizens are affected by his manipulations, and Mark Twain is obviously exhibiting "the damned human race." It is the acquisitive instinct, the greed for wealth, that is involved in this probing of humanity's

From *Mark Twain as a Literary Artist,* pp. 308-309. Copyright © 1950 by the University of Oklahoma Press, publishing division of the university. Reprinted by permission (title is editor's).

frailty. The stranger controls the action of the characters by building up a certain set of circumstances to which he knows they will respond as one man: they have no interior motivation, no wills of their own, to save them from the trap which the stranger sets for them, baited by his own knowledge of human greed.

Nevertheless, in spite of his strongly marked deterministic pattern, Mark Twain is unable to eliminate moral judgments from his solution. The characters, thieves and hypocrites as they are, are all held responsible for their acts by way of the derisive condemnation of the audience; and the two old people, the only ones who win the reader's sympathy, likewise hold themselves morally responsible and are so conscience-stricken that they actually die of broken hearts. With such faults of intellection, the wonder is that Mark Twain is able to make the story as powerful as he does. And it has power. But for the thoughtful reader there is a mischief in it that keeps it from being altogether satisfying, though one may not stop to analyze why. The stranger who devises almost-laboratory conditions for the testing of human behavior in Hadleyburg coincides well with Mark Twain's theme of determinism; but the switch to an implied theme of divine justice—the great theme of the judgment of God as it operates through the consciences of Mr. And Mrs. Richards—makes any unity of effect impossible. The unholy glee with which "the house" chants its sardonic joy at the unmasking of the "Nineteeners" echoes through what is in itself an adolescent voice of judgment, confusing and perplexing the reader. There is no continuity of motivation, no steadiness of emotional effect, no philosophical unity to the story. In it the moralist gives an out-of-bounds blow to the determinist, and Hadleyburg settles itself on a philosophic quicksand.

CLINTON S. BURHANS, JR.
THE SOBER AFFIRMATION OF MARK TWAIN'S "HADLEYBURG"

To say that "The Man That Corrupted Hadleyburg" is one of Twain's finest and most significant works would probably provoke little argument among serious students of his writing. Curiously, however, there are almost no independent studies of this story, and where it is considered in general studies of Twain's art, it is usually given little more than passing attention as a cynical and pessimistic story reflecting the deepening despair of his later years. I think the story deserves more serious consideration by Twain critics, and I offer this essay as a beginning.

Praising the Hadleyburg story, A. B. Paine calls it "a tale that in its own way takes its place with the half-dozen great English short stories of the world," and DeLancey Ferguson declares that while "the short story, as an art form, was not Mark's metier . . . in 'The Man That Corrupted Hadleyburg' he came near to perfection." In contrast, Gladys Bellamy, though recognizing the story's power, feels that "for the thoughtul reader there is a mischief in it that keeps it from being altogether satisfying." She considers the story marred by inconsistencies stemming from two conflicting characteristics of Twain's mind—his determinism and his moralism. Twain, she says, establishes a deterministic framework to explain the motivation and behavior of his characters and then violates it illogically with "an implied theme of divine justice—the great theme of the judgment of God as it operates through the consciences of Mr. and Mrs. Richards. . . . There is no continuity of motivation, no steadiness of emotional effect, no philosophical unity to the story. In it the moralist gives an out-of-bounds blow to the determinist, and Hadleyburg settles itself on a philosophic quicksand."

It seems to me, however, that Miss Bellamy's usually brilliant insight fails her here, for in this story Twain is consistent both logically and aesthetically. On the surface, the story is an attack on human greed and hypocrisy, but at its deeper levels it reflects Twain's return to the unresolved problems which had perplexed him in Huck Finn's moral conflict and an exploration of the possibility that experience can unify man's moral perceptions and his motivating emotions. In this context, Twain's concept of determinism, especially environmental determinism, or training, does not conflict with his moralism; on the contrary, his moralism functions here in terms of his determinism. Moreover, his view of conscience in this story is not, as Miss Bellamy implies, that of the conventional religious moralist; it is far more complicated than this, synthesizing as it does the principal elements in his earlier concepts of conscience.

Twain's determinism in "The Man That Corrupted Hadleyburg," far from being inconsistent with his moralism, is the source of its real values. In his concern in this story with the relations between conscience and the heart, he views the moral values of conscience as determined by environment, by training; and one of his major aims is to show that such training in moral values must be empirical, not merely prescriptive. The people of Hadleyburg try to preserve the honesty which has made them famous by

From *American Literature,* 34 (Nov. 1962), 375-384. Copyright © 1962 by Duke University Press. Reprinted by permission of Duke University Press.

training it into their young. They forget, however, that originally this honesty was not just an abstract ideal, but a principle developed and maintained empirically in constant action against the forces and temptations of dishonesty and therefore rooted by experience firmly among the motivating impulses of the heart. "It was many years ago," Twain writes. "Hadleyburg was the most honest and upright town in all the region around about. It had kept that reputation unsmirched during three generations, and was prouder of it than of any other of its possessions" (p. 351).

So proud are the people of Hadleyburg of their reputation and so fearful of the slightest threat to it that they try to safeguard it not by the continued practice of honesty but rather by an attempt to exclude all temptations to dishonesty. The town "was so proud of it," Twain declares, "and so anxious to insure its perpetuation, that it began to teach the principles of honest dealing to its babies in the cradle, and made the like teachings the staple of their culture thenceforward through all the years devoted to their education. Also, throughout the formative years temptations were kept out of the way of the young people, so that their honesty could have every chance to harden and solidify, and become a part of their very bone" (pp. 351-352). Hadleyburg has tried to create an environment in which the principles of honesty can be trained into the young without the dangers involved in practicing them against inimical temptations. The fame of the town, the people feel, will thereby be secure.

But Hadleyburg's training is defective and artificial on at least two counts: in the first place, it is impossible to shield men forever from all temptations to dishonesty, and when inexorably they do arise, men unpracticed in recognizing and resisting them will succumb, as Richards does in failing to clear Burgess—a failure which foreshadows the fall of Hadleyburg. And in the second place, Hadleyburg forgets that man is determined by heredity as well as by environment, that human nature is potentially petty and selfish as well as noble and kind. Thus, when the town becomes obsessed with vanity over its empty and now unearned reputation, its preoccupation with preserving that reputation by excluding the temptations to dishonesty not only fails but also leaves other vices free to develop unchecked. When Richards tells his wife that " 'we have been trained all our lives long, like the whole village, till it is absolutely second nature to us to stop not a single moment to think when there's an honest thing to be done,' " she refutes him prophetically:

Oh, I know it, I know it—it's been one everlasting training and training and training in honesty—honesty shielded, from the very cradle, against every possible temptation, and so it's *artificial* honesty, and weak as water when temptation comes, as we have seen this night. God knows I never had shade nor shadow of a doubt of my petrified and indestruct-

ible honesty until now—and now, under the very first big and real temptation, I—Edward, it is my belief that this town's honesty is as rotten as
mine is; as rotten as yours is. It is a mean town, a hard, stingy town, and
hasn't a virtue in the world but this honesty it is so celebrated for and
so conceited about; and so help me, I do believe that if ever the day
comes that its honesty falls under great temptation, its grand reputation
will go to ruin like a house of cards. There, now, I've made confession,
and I feel better; I am a humbug, and I've been one all my life, without
knowing it (pp. 360–361).

Obsessive vanity and insulated disuse, then, have made Hadleyburg's
honesty artificial and hypocritical: much like Huck Finn's attitude toward
slavery, it is largely an untested abstraction; it is almost entirely divorced
from the townspeople's hearts. In short, the training of the people of
Hadleyburg has shaped their consciences to an awareness of the moral
ideal of honesty, but it has given them no experience in following the
directions of conscience and therefore no true knowledge of its values.

Seeing in the people of Hadleyburg what they cannot see in themselves,
or, like the Richardses, see too late, the vindictive stranger directs his
ingenious revenge at their most vulnerable spot—the greed for wealth and
social position in hearts whose inexperience in resisting temptations to
dishonesty has left them no answering passion for true honesty. That
Hadleyburg falls, that all of the Nineteen succumb, is therefore not surprising. Nor is their subsequent sense of guilt, as reflected in the
Richardses, at all inconsistent. Both are corollaries of Twain's concept of
determinism; ironically, paradoxically, Hadleyburg's fall is determined
by the abstract training which the people had counted on to keep them
forever incorruptible; and their consciences, whose moral perceptions
also stem from that training, cause them to feel guilt and shame.

In the end, of course, Hadleyburg learns the meaning of its mistakes:
that only through experience can the moral perceptions of conscience be
united with the emotions which motivate man. Moreover, this is also the
significance of the story's central conflict as Twain develops it through the
Richardses. From the beginning he defines this conflict largely in terms of
the relationship between the Richardses' consciences and their hearts,
an evolving relationship synthesizing most of his earlier concepts of
conscience.

At times, Richards's conscience operates like Tom Sawyer's; that is, it
makes moral distinctions and influences him to commensurate action.
Learning that the town is planning to punish the Rev. Burgess for something which only Richards knows he did not do, Richards warns him.
"'When the thing was new and hot,'" he tells his wife, "'and the town
made a plan to ride him on a rail, my conscience hurt me so that I couldn't

stand it, and I went privately and gave him notice, and he got out of the town and staid out till it was safe to come back' " (pp. 9-10). But Richards's training in honesty has been only prescriptive, and his conscience affects his actions only to the point at which they conflict with the desire for the good opinion of the town, which is the principal element in his basic emotion of self-approval. He warns Burgess privately, and almost at once regrets having saved him; he fears the town will find out and turn its dislike of Burgess against him. For, as Twain points out in the contemporaneous *What is Man?*, "Corn-Pone Opinions," and "The United States of Lyncherdom," "the Sole Impulse which dictates and compels a man's every act: the imperious necessity of securing his own approval, in every emergency and at all costs," usually involves not only the disposition to do whatever will gain public approval but also "man's commonest weakness, his aversion to being unpleasantly conspicuous, pointed at, shunned as being on the unpopular side."

Reflecting Hadleyburg's defective training in honesty, Richards's moral ideals are in this crisis almost entirely separated from his motivating emotion of self-approval. In addition to making him regret having saved Burgess, this basic emotion violates his conscience and prevents him from clearing the clergyman of the unjust accusation against him. " 'I am ashamed,' " Richards admits. " 'I was the only man who knew he was innocent. I could have saved him, and—and—well, you know how the town was wrought up—I hadn't the pluck to do it. I would have turned everybody against me. I felt mean, ever so mean; but I didn't dare; I hadn't the manliness to face that' " (p. 356). Here, then, though its moral values and demands as well as the emotions it contends with are the reverse of Huck Finn's, Richards's conscience functions much like Huck's in that it exerts almost no influence on his actions but does punish him with a sense of guilt when he fails to obey it.

The stranger's bag of gold evokes in the Richardses and in the rest of the Nineteen the same conflict between the moral guidance and the demands of their consciences and the urgings of their emotions. Despite the warnings of his conscience, each is driven by his desires for wealth, security, and social position to rationalize and then to lie about his right to the gold. "All night long," Twain writes, "eighteen principal citizens did what their caste-brother Richards was doing at the same time—they put in their energies trying to remember what notable service it was that they had unconsciously done Barclay Goodson. In no case was it a holiday job; still they succeeded" (p. 368). Like Adam and Eve in Twain's version of their temptation and fall, the Nineteen "could not understand untried things and verbal abstractions which stood for matters outside of their little world and their narrow experience" as he wrote in *Europe and Elsewhere*.

The town meeting reveals the dishonesty of the rest of the Nineteen, but for the Richardses it means only more temptation and further conflict between the values and entreaties of their consciences and their passion for public favor. Twice again they are tempted and twice again they fall. When they think their dishonesty is going to be disclosed, they rise to confess and to plead for the town's forgiveness; but when the generous Burgess silences them and then fails to read Richards's note, they are "faint with joy and surprise" and no longer disposed to confess. " 'Oh, bless God,' " whispers Mary Richards, " 'we are saved!—he has lost ours—I wouldn't give this for a hundred of those sacks!' " (p. 381) Their desire for public approval completely overcomes the demands of their consciences that they confess and justly "suffer with the rest" (p. 381), and once more they succumb to the temptation to dishonesty.

Nor is this all, for they compound their dishonesty when the town proposes to auction off the stranger's bag of gold and give the proceeds to them. Again, their consciences point out the Richardses' deceitfulness and urge them to confess: "at the beginning of the auction," Twain writes, "Richards whispered in distress to his wife: 'O Mary, can we allow it? It—it—you see, it is an honor-reward, a testimonial to purity of character, and—and—can we allow it? Hadn't I better get up and—O Mary, what ought we to do?—' " She, too, understands the moral implications and requirements of their position and replies, " 'It is another temptation, Edward—I'm all in a tremble—but, oh, we've escaped *one* temptation, and that ought to warn us to— . . . O Edward . . . we are *so* poor!—but—but—do as you think best—do as you think best.' " This, however, is precisely what he does not do; "Edward fell," Twain declares, "—that is, he sat still; sat with a conscience which was not satisfied, but which was overpowered by circumstances" (pp. 384-385), circumstances of wealth and an intoxicating public admiration.

As the incitements to dishonesty become more tempting, then, conscience in the Richardses, as in the Hadleyburg they reflect, diminishes as an effective moral and ethical force; and finally, much as Twain defines it in *What Is Man?*, it has no moral and ethical function at all. For a while the consciences they have violated cause the Richardses to feel some last glimmerings of guilt and shame and regret: Richards decides to resign his position at the bank, feeling that he can no longer trust himself with other people's money; and both he and his wife are made profoundly miserable by Stephenson's note praising their honesty. But these feelings soon die, and the Richardses' sense of guilt becomes a matter not of morality but of exposure; "within twenty-four hours after the Richardses had received their checks," Twain writes, "their consciences were quieting down, discouraged; the old couple were learning to reconcile themselves to the sin which they had committed. But they were to learn, now, that a sin takes on new and real terrors when there seems a chance that it is going to be found out. This gives it a fresh and most substantial and important aspect" (p. 390).

Fearing the exposure of their dishonesty, the Richardses are no longer concerned with the moral values and responsibilities of their situation. The separation between their ideal of honesty and their motivating emotions is now complete, and their consciences lose all moral and ethical function and become in effect identical with the Richardses' self-approval in its passion for public approval. Conscience now moves the Richardses only to a suspicion that others know about their dishonesty and to fear that someone will disclose it, particularly the suspicion that Burgess knows of Richards's failure long ago to reveal his innocence and the fear that he intends to revenge himself by exposing them.

Tortured beyond endurance, the Richardses sicken and die, but not from any Divine punishment reflected in the agonies of a guilty conscience. They die because they cannot abide the knowledge that their good name may be destroyed and that they may be held up to an even greater obloquy than the rest of the Nineteen. In short, they are no longer aware of sin and guilt as matters of moral principle and individual responsibility; self-approval is their conscience, and its demand for public favor renders them obsessed, like the town they mirror, with the name of honesty at the cost of its essence, which would mean, as Richards realizes in the town meeting, confessing publicly that they have been as dishonest as the others.

Before the Richardses die, however, Twain reveals that they have not suffered barrenly. Their racking fear that their dishonesty will be exposed has rooted the knowledge of that dishonesty deeply in their hearts; through experience, the self-approval which is their conscience has learned moral and ethical responsibility and now makes moral distinctions which result in commensurate action. In Richards, as Twain in *Huck Finn* implies they must, conscience and the heart, moral perception and motivating emotion, at last function together. Richards's ideal of honesty is rooted in his heart, in the self-approval which governs his actions, and he dies an honest man.

Concerned anew with moral values, he destroys the checks which have cost him so dearly; " 'they came from Satan,' " he tells the nurse. " 'I saw the hell-brand on them, and I knew they were sent to betray me to sin' " (p. 391). His self-approval now demands behavior consistent with moral rectitude, and he wants the essence of honesty, not its mere reputation. With his last breath, he admits his guilt—not privately, as in what he had told his wife about Burgess, but openly in a public avowal. " 'I want witnesses,' " he declares. "I want you all to hear my confession, so that I may die a man, and not a dog. I was clean—artificially—like the rest; and like the rest I fell when temptation came. I signed a lie, and claimed the miserable sack'" (p. 392). Moreover, though he thinks Burgess has exposed him, Richards admits his cowardly failure to save the clergyman from undeserved disgrace.

Experience has made Richards's conscience a highly complex faculty in which moral perception and direction and the motivating emotion of self-approval work together to produce real honesty—honesty which is not simply allegiance to an abstract principle, but honesty expressed in practice against the temptations of dishonesty. Nor is this lesson lost upon Hadleyburg, which learns fully and well what the Nineteen and particularly the Richardses exemplify: the town's new motto, "Lead Us Into Temptation," is not an invitation to sin, but a means to grapple with it empirically. Whatever its new name may be, Hadleyburg is truly "an honest town once more, and the man will have to rise early that catches it napping again" (p. 393).

"The Man That Corrupted Hadleyburg" is therefore neither as inconsistent nor as pessimistic as it is usually considered. In it are reflected the major aspects of Twain's conflicting moral thought—moral values as abstract, moral values as empirical; conscience as the reflector of moral values, conscience as the amoral emotion of self-approval—but these conflicting ideas are reconciled by Twain's determinism into a formal and thematic unity which generates substantial beauty and power. Moreover, the story is in fact less pessimistic than soberly optimistic; it ends, after all, not with the greed, hypocrisy, and cynicism of the town meeting, but with the development of a significant conscience in Richards and in the affirmation of Hadleyburg's new motto. And if Twain shows man as a deterministic creature driven by vanity and greed, he also shows that this is neither the complete nor the final answer to the question of man, that the experience of living can determine man to his salvation as well as to his perdition.

In "The Man That Corrupted Hadleyburg," then, Twain declares with Milton that "I cannot praise a fugitive and cloistered virtue, unexercised and unbreathed, that never sallies out and sees her adversary, but slinks out of the race where that immortal garland is to be run for, not without dust and heat. Assuredly we bring not innocence into the world, we bring impurity much rather: that which purifies us is trial, and trial is by what is contrary. That virtue therefore which is but a youngling in the contemplation of evil, and knows not the utmost that vice promises to her followers, and rejects it, is but a blank virtue, not a pure; her whiteness is but an excremental whiteness. . . ." Again, Twain argues with Conrad's

Stein [in *Lord Jim*] that " 'the way is to the destructive element submit yourself, and with the exertions of your hands and feet in the water make the deep, deep sea keep you up. . . . In the destructive element immerse . . . .' " In "The Man That Corrupted Hadleyburg," Twain's divergent moral and ethical ideas merge in a view of man which places Twain within a great and positive tradition.

HENRY NASH SMITH
TWAIN'S MATHEMATICAL DEMONSTRATION OF
HUMAN GREED

"The Man That Corrupted Hadleyburg" treats the theme of human bondage in an almost algebraic fashion. The central character is Richards, cashier of the bank in a small town faintly reminiscent of Hannibal even though the local color has been almost entirely sweated out of it. There is no reference to Negro slavery—the time is late nineteenth century—but Richards calls himself a "slave" to the bank president Pinkerton, and all the leading citizens, including Pinkerton, are enslaved by greed. Their love of money contrasts ironically with the town's self-righteous pride in its reputation for honesty, that is, "commercial incorruptibility." The story concentrates on the hollowness of this outward show of rectitude, bringing together once again the themes of training and of the contrast between appearance and reality.

The demonstration that the elite of Hadleyburg is not honest, but basically corrupt, is undertaken by an outsider who is fleetingly assimilated to the group of Mark Twain's literary sleuths: on the only occasion when his appearance is described he resembles "an amateur detective gotten up like an impossible English earl." Like Pudd'nhead Wilson, although by a different method, he reveals the truth beneath the facade of the town's respectability. His motive is vengeance for some undisclosed offense against him by a resident of Hadleyburg—a motive that, together with his aura of mystery, causes him to resemble the Deity in Mark Twain's later thought. In order to demonstrate that greed is universal in "poor, tempted, and mistrained" humanity, he leaves in the village a bag

From *Mark Twain: The Development of a Writer* (Cambridge, Mass.: Belknap Press of Harvard University Press), pp. 183-184. Copyright © 1962 by the President and Fellows of Harvard College. Reprinted by permission (title is editor's).

supposed to contain a fortune in gold coins. At the same time he sends anonymous letters to nineteen prominent citizens saying the money is to be given to an unknown benefactor who can identify himself by recalling what he said when he gave money on a certain occasion to a stranger in distress. The cynical device works: in nineteen households the same process of rationalization begins, the same conversations take place between husband and wife, and an effect of sardonic comedy is achieved by the choreographic automatism. Through close attention to Richards and his wife Mark Twain reveals in scathing detail the methods by which human beings conceal their motives from themselves.

A boisterous town meeting makes public eighteen identical efforts to get the money by means of fabricated evidence. Richards, however, is spared for a worse torment. The minister Burgess protects him by suppressing the fraudulent note that Richards, along with the other men tempted by the stranger, has submitted in support of his claim to the money. Richards succumbs again to the more grievous temptation of being publicly acclaimed for his integrity, receives a fortune together with the praise of the community, and dies from the pangs of guilt and shame. It is hard to conceive of a more tightly mathematical demonstration of human depravity.

A faint suggestion that the humble ones of this earth may be free of the compulsions binding the upper class is provided by Jack Halliday, "the loafing, good-natured, no-account irreverent fisherman, hunter, boys' friend, stray-dogs' friend" who mocks the leading citizens. But Mark Twain has so little interest in Halliday that he forgets the vernacular precedents in his own work and calls him the "typical 'Sam Lawson' of the town"—invoking as a model a character in Mrs. Stowe's *Oldtown Folks* who is portrayed from the patronizing viewpoint of local-color writing.

Hadleyburg is Dawson's Landing [the setting of *Pudd'nhead Wilson*] without either the intimations of evil radiating from the character of Tom Driscoll or the vivid thrust of Roxy's passion. It is not tragic, even potentially, but merely smug and hypocritical. The story nevertheless attains a considerable distinction by its tightness of construction, its evenness of tone, and its hard, spare prose. Mark Twain's mastery of a style based on oral speech but fined down to an instrument of precision survived the collapse of his power to create full-bodied characters or complex fictive worlds.

HENRY B. RULE

THE ROLE OF SATAN IN
"THE MAN THAT CORRUPTED HADLEYBURG"

"I have always felt friendly toward Satan," Twain wrote in his *Autobiography.* "Of course that is ancestral; it must be in the blood, for I could not have originated it." Perhaps it was "ancestral," for Twain described in another passage of his *Autobiography* his mother's sympathy for Satan. He wasn't "treated fairly," she claimed. After all, he was just a sinner, like the rest of us. Sinful man cannot save himself by his own efforts; his hope lies in "the mighty help of pathetic, appealing, imploring prayers that go up daily out of all the Churches in Christendom and out of myriads upon myriads of pitying hearts. But," she asked, "who prays for Satan?" It is doubtful that Jane Clemens caused many of her fellow Presbyterians to relent in their hardened attitudes toward Satan. But her son, Sam, apparently heard her and decided to do something about this injustice. In his article, "Is Shakespeare Dead?" Twain said that when he was seven years old he asked his Sunday-school teacher, Mr. Barclay, a stone-mason, to tell him about Satan. Mr. Barclay was willing to set forth the five or six facts concerning Satan's history, "but he stopped there; he wouldn't allow any discussion of them." Upon hearing that Sam was thinking about a biography of Satan, Mr. Barclay was "shocked" and made the boy stop writing. Mr. Barclay's victory was temporary, however, for Twain never relinquished his determination to become Satan's biographer. Among his writings in which Satan plays the lead role are "Letters to Satan," "Sold to Satan," "A Humane Word for Satan," "Letters from Earth," "That Day in Eden," and the two major works of his old age—"The Man that Corrupted Hadleyburg" and *The Mysterious Stranger.*

Twain's interest in Satan bore its most remarkable fruit in the year 1898. In that year he avowed his determination to rehabilitate Satan's character, began the first version of *The Mysterious Stranger,* and finished "The Man That Corrupted Hadleyburg." His resolution to rescue Satan from centuries of slander was candidly expressed in his article "Concerning the Jews." In this article Twain declared that he had "no prejudice" against Satan and admitted that he even leaned "a little his way, on account of his not having a fair show": "All religions issue bibles against him, and say the most injurious things about him, but we never hear *his*

From *Studies in Short Fiction,* 6 (Fall 1969), 619-629. Reprinted by permission of the author and the editor of *Studies.*

side. We have none but the evidence for the prosecution, and yet we have rendered the verdict. . . . As soon as I can get at the facts I will undertake his rehabilitation myself, if I can find an unpolitic publisher." Acting upon his determination to restore Satan's character, Twain jotted in his notebook the plot outline for the first version of *The Mysterious Stranger:* "Story of little Satan Jr. who came to Hannibal, went to school, was popular and greatly liked by those who knew his secret. The others were jealous and the girls didn't like him because he smelled of brimstone. He was always doing miracles—his pals knew they were miracles. The others thought they were mysteries." The final version of *The Mysterious Stranger* was laid in a sixteenth-century Austrian village rather than in the Hannibal of Twain's youth. But for his best Satan story, "The Man That Corrupted Hadleyburg," Twain *did* return to the scene of his earlier masterpieces—the small village in the American hinterland—only this time the innocent vision of boyhood is supplanted (there are no children in "Hadleyburg") by the disillusioned gaze of adulthood.

A good deal of critical attention has focused on the ethical and philosophical import of "Hadleyburg," but little on its allegorical ingenuity, and to miss this aspect of the story is to miss much of its satirical and moral force. The purpose of this essay is to examine "Hadleyburg" as another example of the Eden myth that, as R. W. B. Lewis in his *The American Adam* has demonstrated, is so prominent in the American literary tradition. When one recognizes that "the mysterious stranger" in the story is Satan, then Hadleyburg becomes an ironic Eden that is diseased by hypocrisy and money-lust—an Eden that is symbolic of the fallen hopes of the American forefathers for a new paradise on Earth where mankind could begin afresh in peace and brotherhood and Godliness. In Twain's treatment of the Eden myth, Satan plays the role of savior rather than corrupter. The Eden of Hadleyburg, microcosm of America, is already corrupted by greed and deceit before Satan arrives on the scene. Although his initial motivation may have been revenge, the result of Satan's machinations is to lead Hadleyburg, perhaps without his volition, to some degree of moral reformation.

The character of the stranger in "Hadleyburg" is the same as that of Satan in the Bible and in folklore. His *strangeness,* his nonhuman difference, is suggested at the beginning of the story by a repetition of the word *stranger.* Hadleyburg "had the ill luck to offend a passing stranger" (p. 352). Mrs. Richards is "afraid of the mysterious big stranger" when he enters her house (p. 353). He introduces himself to her with the words, "I am a stranger" (p. 353). In the letter that he leaves with her, he declares, "I am a foreigner," (p. 353) and his confession as to why ("made as I am") (p. 383) he cannot gain his revenge by merely killing the citizens of

Hadleyburg also stresses his foreignness or strangeness. In the past, he was "a ruined gambler" (p. 353)—a reference to the greatest gamble of all time, Satan's foiled rebellion against Jehovah; he even thinks in gambling terms: "Yes, he saw my deuces *and* with a straight flush, and by rights the pot is his" (p. 385). Now, his home is in Mexico (p. 364), land of fiery heat, and he is several times associated with hell-fire. When he arrived at his plan to corrupt Hadleyburg, his whole head was "lit up with an evil joy" (p. 352); and the guilty Richards remarks upon receving a note from him, "It seems written with fire—it burns so" (p. 389). Like the Satan in the Book of Job, he is a wanderer ("all through his wanderings") (p. 352). Like the Satan in Genesis, he is the master of disguises; the disguise that he chooses for his appearance at the town-hall meeting ("an impossible English earl") (p. 385) suggests Prince Satan's aristocratic lineage as does also the name Stephenson (Greek *stephanos,* a crown) that he signs to the letter addressed to the nineteen principal citizens of Hadleyburg.

His dominion over Hadleyburg (Hadesburg?) is Satanic in its method and extent. He is the trickster and schemer of Christian and biblical fame. This "bitter man and revengeful" spent "a whole year" laying his snare for the men of Hadleyburg (p. 352). He is the father of lies who leads Richards to tell his first lie to his wife and who unmasks the lie that the whole town had been living. He is the tempter who speeds Hadleyburg to its fall by the lure of gold, for he knows that in Hadleyburg "the love of money is the root of all evil"; as he slyly tells the citizens at the town-hall meeting, "I have dealings with persons interested in numismatics all over the world" (p. 385). The ease with which he manipulates the Hadley-burgians through their greed proves him to be "the ruler of this world" (John, 12:31). The town-hall meeting is "the synagogue of Satan" (Rev. 2:9) or the Devil's Mass of Christian folklore: "The house droned out the eight words in a massed and measured and musical deep volume of sound (with a daringly close resemblance to a well-known church chant)," ending with "a grand and agonized and imposing 'A-a-a-a-men!'" (p. 381). The pious folk of Hadleyburg have given themselves over to Satan and have become his "children."

The names of the other main characters suggest their symbolic roles in Twain's fable. Richards's name implies that he is a "son of riches" who yearns for the wealth of his master, Pinkerton the banker. His first words in the story disclose his envy of Pinkerton: " 'I'm so tired—tired clear out; it is dreadful to be poor, and to make these dismal journeys at my time of life. Always at the grind, grind, on a salary—another man's slave, and he sitting at home in his slippers, rich and comfortable' " (p. 354). Even his given name Edward (Anglo-Saxon *ead* riches and *weard* guardian= guardian of riches) suggests his social status as well as his occupation at the bank. On the other hand, Twain places the Reverend Mr. Burgess (historically, his name denotes a freeman of a borough who owed special duties to the king and had special privileges) somewhere in between the position of those within the boundaries of Hadleyburg society, like the Richardses, and a true outsider, like Jack Halliday. His speech at the town meeting shows that he believes in the shibboleths of Hadleyburg, and as a minister he had held in the past an important position in society. But the fact that he has been cast out of Hadleyburg society because of the accusation of some crime that he didn't commit allows him a certain freedom from the narrow code of Hadleyburg, and he is able to perform the virtuous and sacrificial act of perjuring himself in order to save the Richardses from disgrace. Jack Halliday's name connotes his freedom from the pressures of Hadleyburg's business community. He is the only man in town who maintains a "holiday" mood as he jokes and laughs at the principal citizens throughout their vacillations from "holy happiness" (p. 363) to sad and sick reverie. Apparently, he was born outside of Hadleyburg respectability. He is a kind of "natural" man or grown-up Huck Finn, this "loafing, good-natured, no-account, irreverent fisherman, hunter, boys' friend, stray-dogs' friend" (p. 362). It is ironic that these two outsiders—the ruined minister and the no-account loafer—are chosen to be the leaders of the town-meeting, a tribute to their moral superiority.

The name of Goodson (God's son) reveals his role as Christ in the world of Hadleyburg. His alienation from society is due neither to force nor to birth, but to his own moral conviction. He is the most hated man in town, for he sees through its sanctimonious cant. But everyone knows privately that he is the "one good generous soul in this village" (p. 365), and Satan points out (while making a pun) that he was the only man in Hadleyburg who "would give away twenty dollars to a poor devil" (p. 383). If we keep in mind the significance of Goodson's name, then the attempt of Richards (the son of riches) to save the soul of Goodson (the son of God) becomes highly ironic. Goodson's moral force, mysterious origin, and spiritual destination are suggested when Satan admits that at first he was afraid that Goodson might mar his plan to corrupt Hadleyburg, for "he was neither born nor reared in Hadleyburg. . . . But heaven took Goodson." Goodson's propertyless state and the hatred of the village philistines for him are also in the Christ tradition, but his defiance and bitterness do not conform to the character of the meek and loving Christ in the Gospels. However "years and years ago" (as long ago as 2,000 years?) he had been a man of love rather than hate. In his youth, Goodson had been in love with a girl named Nancy Hewitt, but "the match had been broken off; the girl died"; and Goodson became "a frank despiser of the human species" (p. 367). The etymology of the sweetheart's name—Nancy (diminutive-variant of

Anna, from the Hebrew *hannah,* grace) Hewitt (diminutive-variant of Hugh, Teutonic for spirit) reveals the spiritual or heavenly quality of Goodson's love. Twain strongly suggests in the story that the broken engagement and the girl's death were due to the village gossip "that she carried a spoonful of negro blood in her veins." The love of Goodson for this racially mixed girl, therefore, recalls the love of "the heavenly bridegroom" for mankind in general, and the broken engagement and the death of the girl may represent Twain's despairing conviction that the love of Christ is doomed in the world of Hadleyburg. "God's son" has gone to heaven, and Satan has a clear field.

The true god of the Hadleyburgians is Mammon, one of Satan's chieftains, not the God of love to whom they pray in church. The piety of Mrs. Richards, who plays the role of Eve in Twain's allegory of the Fall, is completely ineffectual as protection against the golden temptation of Satan. When Satan knocks on her door, she is piously reading the *Missionary Herald,* but as soon as he leaves her alone with the gold-sack, her tranquility is shattered. At first she weakly struggles against its fatal attraction and mutters a few prayers, but she soon finds herself kneeling in worship at the golden altar of Satan: "She turned the light down low, and slipped steathily over and kneeled down by the sack and felt of its ridgy sides with her hands, and fondled them lovingly; and there was a gloating light in her poor old eyes" (p. 358).

The picture of poor Mrs. Richards kneeling before the sack of gilded coins is a blistering satire on the place of wealth in the Protestant fundamentalism of the citizens of Hadleyburg. Twain depicts the gross adulteration of virtue by money, piety by wealth, in the minds of these pious folk with beautiful irony in their unconscious language. "What a fortune for the kind man who set his bread afloat upon the waters!" exclaims Mrs. Richards upon reading Satan's first letter (p. 354). In his speech to his townspeople, Rev. Burgess unwittingly accentuates the relationship between piety and profit in the minds of the Hadleyburgians by his mixture of Christian and commercial terminology. The town's "reputation" for honesty, he declares, is "a treasure of priceless value," and he predicts that "under Providence its value will become inestimably enhanced." He then rises to a climax: "Today there is not a person who could be beguiled to touch a penny not his own—see to it that you abide in this grace." And the audience responds, "We will! We will!" The religious words *providence* and *grace* acquire a new ironic intensity when one recognizes that they refer to the guidance and inspiration, not of God, but of Satan. Satan is the ruler of Hadleyburg. The irony becomes even more sardonic when, in a parody of the Puritan doctrine of inherited sin, the minister urges his townspeople to transmit their reputation "to your children and to your children's children" (p. 371).

Fallen Hadleyburg is a microcosm of fallen America. Rather than the new Canaan, the Kingdom of God in the wilderness that the forefathers had envisioned, America had become the new Babylonia devoted to the golden altar of Mammon. "I am grateful to America for what I have received at her hands during my long stay under her flag" (p. 353), confesses Satan with a fine sense of irony. The scene at the beginning of the town-hall meeting (or Devil's mass) constitutes an acid satire on American greed. Flags—emblems of national honor and pride—are everywhere. "The platform at the end of the hall was backed by a showy draping of flags: at intervals along the walls were festoons of flags; the gallery fronts were clothed in flags; the supporting columns were swathed in flags; all of this," says Twain in what appears to be a pun, "was to impress the stranger [*i.e.,* Satan], for he would be there in considerable force, and in a large degree he would be connected with the press" (p. 370). (Twain's low opinion of newspapers is well known). At the center of this patriotic display sits the gold-sack "on a little table at the front of the platform where all the house could see it." The whole audience rivets its attention on it "with a burning interest, a mouth-watering interest, a wistful and pathetic interest . . . tenderly, lovingly, proprietarily . . ." (pp. 370-371). The scene is a brilliant satire on national avarice; and what makes the satire even more effective is the revelation that the "gold" discs are lead covered with gilt—a perfect symbol for the falsity of what Twain called "the gilded age" and its pursuits.

The one thing in this ironic Eden of Hadleyburg that is more precious than gold is the town's "reputation" for honesty. The false and empty pride of Hadleyburg in its honesty represents the apple that Eve plucked— "the very apple of your eye" (p. 383), as Satan described it to the Hadleyburgians—and anticipates its fall. Hadleyburg values its reputation for honesty mainly for business reasons: "the mere fact that a young man hailed from Hadleyburg was all the recommendation he needed when he went forth from his natal town to seek for responsible employment" (p. 352). The true substance of Hadleyburg's honesty is indicated by Mrs. Richards's words as soon as she realizes that she is alone with a sack of gold: "Mercy on us, and the door not locked!" (p. 353). Filled with anxiety, she flies about locking the door and pulling down window shades. It is their reputation for honesty that the Hadleyburgians treasure, not its reality. Some of the most cutting ironies in the story spring from the incongruity between private deed and public appearance. When Satan at the town-meeting speaks of the "invulnerable probity" of the Richardses, they "blush prettily; however," Twain adds sardonically, "it went for modesty, and did no harm" (p. 385). Any act is permissible as long as it is performed in the dark. "Oh, bless God, we are saved!" cries Mrs. Richards when Burgess fails to read their test-remark (p. 381). Salvation for these pious people consists of keeping their sins hidden from public view. Edward Richards is so fearful of public opinion that he repents of his one act of virtue—his warning to Burgess of the town's plan to ride him on a rail. "Edward!" gasps his wife Mary. "If the town had found it out—" "Don't! It scares me yet to think it. I repented of it the minute it was done" (p. 357). Obviously, the apple (*i.e.,* Hadleyburg "honesty") in this Eden is ready to drop from the weight of its own corruption. Satan's purpose is to force the inhabitants to eat this bitter fruit of their hypocrisy.

To accomplish this aim, that master engineer, Satan, manipulates his weak and foolish Edenites with superhuman precision. The mechanical actions of the dog in the audience at the town-hall is an amusing image of the automatic reflexes of the Hadleyburgians to Satan's relentless stratagems: when the crowd rises to its feet, so does the dog; when the crowd roars, the dog barks "itself crazy" (pp. 378, 384, 386). The Richardses constantly have the feeling that their actions are controlled by a force outside of themselves, but they are too weak to resist. "Do you think we are to blame, Edward—*much* to blame?" Mary asks. "We—we couldn't help it, Mary. It—well, it was ordered. All things are" (p. 387). Edwards answers truthfully enough, although he would have been shocked to know that his actions were "ordered" by Satan, not God. Man is nothing more than a machine that responds automatically according to outside stimuli—this is the philosophy of man described in Twain's "bible," *What is Man?* written the same year as "Hadleyburg," and in many respects an enlightening commentary on the short story. Satan has no need to perform crude miracles; all he has to do is to activate the human mechanism with the desire for wealth and the need for the approval of his fellows and set it on its track. Each human piston goes through its cycles with perfect timing. When Edward puts on his hat and leaves his house "without a word," he doesn't need to communicate his intentions to his wife: both have arrived at the same conclusion in silence (p. 358). In the meantime, Cox, the newspaper editor, and his wife go through the same series as did the Richardses: elation and pride, fidgety silence, unspoken agreement, and departure. Richards and Cox meet at the foot of the printing-office stairs; again there is no need for words; but Satan has timed their mechanical reflexes so precisely that they meet just two minutes too late to spoil his plan. Later, the rest of the nineteen principal citizens go through the same intricate series of maneuvers as does their "caste brother Richards" (p. 368). Each puppet has been cast in the same mold, and Satan knows exactly which lever to pull or button to push to accomplish his ends.

This picture of robot man is grim and pessimistic, but not without hope. In *What is Man?* Twain states that in man's "chameleonship" lies "his greatest good fortune." The human machine cannot change from within, but the influences that dominate it can be changed. The duty of government, therefore, should be to lay "traps for people. Traps baited with *Initiatory Impulses toward high ideals.*" That is exactly what Satan does in "Hadleyburg": he *traps* his victims into reform. The lies of the Father of Lies are an agency of truth. He weaves a snare of lies about the Hadleyburgians to force them to recognize that they have been living a monstrous lie.

Immediately after Satan sets into motion his machinations, the moral reformation of the Richardses begins. His stratagems lead this pathetic, middle-aged Adam and Eve to know the truth about themselves. Mary, who subscribes to the *Missionary Herald,* is very soon convinced that charity does not begin at *her* home by the realization that her husband lacks the generosity to give "a stranger twenty dollars" (p. 354). They both become aware that the only person in the town capable of an act of much magnanimity was the hated outcast Goodson. Edward must admit to Mary that the town's hostility toward Burgess stems from an injustice and that he hasn't the courage to right the wrong. Stripped of illusions concerning themselves, they can see the town in its true light. "Edward, it is my belief that this town's honesty is as rotten as mine is; as rotten as yours is," Mary confesses (p. 360). Treading the well-worn path of Puritan regeneration, the Richardses are led first to a perception of their own sinfulness and then to a public confession. Whether or not Edward dies in a state of grace, his death-bed confession does have three beneficial results: (1) it enables him to die under the illusion, at least, that he is "a man, and not a dog" (p. 392)—like the automatic dog in the town-hall audience; (2) it at last clears Burgess of the crime that the town had charged against him; and (3) it completes the destruction of the false pride of the town by revealing that its last respected important citizen had also sinned.

It is safe to conclude, therefore, that Satan is Hadleyburg's greatest benefactor. In addition to his arsenal of therapeutic lies, he has one other mighty weapon against humbuggery—laughter. When Satan traps the Hadleyburgians into facing the shattering discrepancy between their pious pretentions and their secret venality, they explode into roars of whole-hearted laughter that sweeps away their hypocrisy. The change of the motto of the town from "Lead us not into temptation" to "Lead us into temptation" proves that the experience had had a lasting effect (p. 393). As Satan in *The Mysterious Stranger* points out: ". . . your race in its poverty has unquestionably one really effective weapon—

laughter. Power, money, persuasion, supplication, persecution—these can lift at a colossal humbug—push it a little—weaken it a little, century by century; but only laughter can blow it to rags and atoms at a blast. Against the assault of laughter nothing can stand." The pious citizens of the town are quite unaware of the ironic application of their chant as Satan leaves the town-hall: "You are f-a-r from being a b-a-a-d man—a-a-a-a-men!" (p. 387). Satan's original motive may have been revenge, but the result of his labors is to bring Hadleyburg to an understanding of its corruption so that it can reform. That he reveres virtue can be seen in his apology to Edward: "I honor you—and that is sincere, too." (p. 389).

Satan as man's benefactor is a fairly common idea in nineteenth-century literature. The cynical Mephistopheles in Goethe's *Faust,* of which Twain owned several translations, is clearly an unwitting servant of God; his duty is to stimulate man's discontent so that he will constantly strive for a higher ideal. Other books that he read—*The Gods* by Robert G. Ingersoll (who was one of Twain's heroes), and *La Sorcière* by Jules Michelet (which Twain probably read in preparation for his *Personal Recollections of Joan of Arc*) defend Satan and his devils as humane and civilizing forces in the world. Most likely, however, Twain's characterization is derived from the Bible, which he had memorized as a boy during many weary Sabbaths. Many Biblical passages depict Satan as a servant of God whose functions are to test man's faith, punish his wickedness, and purge his flesh "that his spirit may be saved" (I Cor. 5:5). Perhaps Satan's major service to man is to chasten his pride. This is the role that he employs to bring about the fortunate fall of the Eden of Hadleyburg. Saint Paul himself was aware of Satan's usefulness as a means of humbling man's pride: "And to keep me from being too elated by the abundance of revelations, a thorn was given me in the flesh, a messenger of Satan, to harass me, to keep me from being too elated" (I Cor. 12:7). Possibly this and similar passages in the Bible, in addition to the encouragement of his kindhearted mother, inspired little Sam at the age of seven to rescue Satan from nineteen centuries of Christian defamation. "Hadleyburg" is the finest product of that long endeavor.

"Hadleyburg" is far superior to *The Mysterious Stranger,* the other major Satan story of Twain's old age. It is more subtle, more wittily devious in its presentation of Satan and mankind and their relation to one another. "Hadleyburg" achieves the unity of tone and aesthetic distance that satire and irony require, while *The Mysterious Stranger* violently alternates between the vulgar antics of a P. T. Barnum side show and the nakedly ferocious tirades of a world-hating, self-hating old man. Twain himself once described [in a letter to Howells] the reason for the artistic failure of *The Mysterious Stranger:* ". . . of course a man can't write successful satire except he be in a calm judicial good-humor . . . in truth I don't ever seem to be in a good enough humor with anything to *satirize* it; no, I want to stand up before it & curse it, & foam at the mouth,—or take a club & pound it to rags & pulp." For once, while writing "Hadleyburg," Twain found the emotional restraint to create a work of art. Standing alone among the products of his old age for the neatness and precision of its form and the richness of its allegorical ironies, "Hadleyburg" might be compared to two other American treatments of the Eden myth—Hawthorne's "Young Goodman Brown" and Melville's *Billy Budd.*

MAXWELL GEISMAR
TWAIN'S IRONIC PARABLE
ON THE HYPOCRISY OF HUMAN VIRTUE

Uneven in craft, rough in detail, "Hadleyburg" is a remarkable story, a fascinating sequel to *Pudd'nhead Wilson,* an important precursor to *The Mysterious Stranger* in the dark vein of Mark Twain's later fables. This western village was really a Hegelian reversal, or contradiction, of Hannibal, Missouri. Its fame was for its "commercial integrity," the moral virtue, the upright honesty and sobriety of its citizens. But who was the "mysterious stranger" himself who, having been wounded by the town, deliberately set out to corrupt it, to prove that all its pretenses of impeccable respectability were a fraud? This was again a dream-nightmare tale with a satanic figure as the mysterious activating presence; this was the dream turned inside out. Its satire followed that of the Virginia aristocrats in *Pudd'nhead,* those FFV's (First Families of Virginia) who were so honorable about everything except their subhuman slaves; and at base "Hadleyburg" was an eloquent example of the corruption of the old American republic by the great booming nineteenth century's notion of "progress."

The tone of the story was not realistic but symbolical, or closer, like *Pudd'nhead,* to a kind of native surrealism which Clemens invented for his own purposes. And "Hadleyburg" was also a brilliant study, psychological

Reprinted from *Mark Twain: An American Prophet* by Maxwell Geismar. Copyright © by Maxwell Geismar. Used by permission of the publisher, Houghton Mifflin Company (title is editor's).

and social, of the influence of money upon the human spirit, or of the prevalence of greed in the human temperament when confronted by temptation. Clemens was projecting his own torment over a decade of financial ruin, surely, but he was projecting it into a specific historical context: the corruption of the town's earlier, more natural and less materialistic human types and social relationships. When the mysterious stranger leaves the sack of gold, poor Mrs. Richards immediately locks the house doors and bars the windows which had previously been open; her first thought is of thieves. The full, open, and easy quality of western frontier existence—the earlier democracy of small means and social equality in the older epochs of the national development—has been lost forever.

"It is dreadful to be poor," says Mr. Richards; but it is much more dreadful for them to be rich. His first thought was to destroy the stranger's written bequest and keep the sack of gold; the virtue of the frontier crumbled under the first temptation. Hadleyburg was indeed an "honest, narrow, self-righteous and stingy" town, as the village rebel, Barclay Goodson, had declared. In these symbolic or surrealist tales, Twain often used rather obvious names for his central figures.

And this is also a story of a terrible moral conformity, a fear of generous or bold human action, a show of public virtue as a mask for private gain, an overwhelming social hypocrisy which covers the contortions of small, if not evil souls.

The Richardses are really a terrible couple whom Clemens described with absolute accuracy; we flinch when we read about them because we understand them so well. The central logic, the developments in the early part of the story, the twists of human temperament and social circumstance alike, are invented by a diabolical intelligence. The greedy cunning of the Richardses is only equaled by their tormented anxiety—not an anxiety about their scheming fancies but as to the possible appearance of their deeds. There is no question of morality in the whole town of Hadleyburg; there is only a question of practical consequences. "God forgive me—it's awful to think such things," says Mary Richards, "but . . . Lord, how we are made—how strangely we are made!"—and her guilt does not prevent her from further manifestations of greed. During the period of his own financial manipulations, Sam Clemens had learned much about the desperate possibilities of the human temperament. "Hadleyburg" is a Balzacian tale of frontier life.

But his financial experiences had added a depth and a bite to Clemens' writing. The foolish artist, as the psychoanalytic critics don't seem to understand, can enrich his art by his folly. And one notices how often the central figures of these stories—the "gambler," the "outcast," the "schemers," the respectable hypocrites—are obvious projections of aspects of Twain's own temperament, now used as his literary pawns.

Mary Richards again admits her guilt. "It is a mean town, a hard, stingy town," and it is her belief that the town's honesty is as rotten as hers is—and still she goes on scheming with her anxiety-ridden husband to get the golden fortune. And the "moral" struggles of the Richardses are repeated by the Coxes and by "Pinkerton," the town banker. And Jack Halliday, who is the loafing, good-natured, no-account, irreverent fisherman, hunter, boys' friend, and bum of the town, Jack Halliday, or Holiday, the pagan Huck Finn character of the story, becomes a kind of a frontier Greek chorus which records the alternation of joy (greed) and depression (fear of financial loss) in the leading townspeople. It develops that the reward will go to the person who knows what the social outcast Goodson told the ruined gambler (the satanic stranger, or doubtless the mask of Sam Clemens himself) which changed his whole life. Everybody is trying to remember—or invent—that remark in order to get the money, in the malicious development of the story.

Each of the "Nineteen," the leading citizens of the town, gets a similar letter; each thinks he is the only recipient of the prize, each concludes he must have some special virtue to deserve this fortune—their only problem is *what* virtue? When Richards gets his clue to the fortune, his wife is ecstatic. "Oh, Edward, the money is ours, and I am so grateful, *oh, so* grateful—kiss me dear, it's forever since we kissed—and we needed it —the money," she cries. Clemens is explicit about the repression of sexual pleasure in the face of financial anxiety.

For if Hadleyburg's had been a false virtue, untested by temptation, it is nevertheless true that the "deadly money" has now destroyed the town's whole social fabric and all its personal relations. Poor Richards— "Poor Richard," and one remembers the deadly animus of Twain's earliest attacks on Benjamin Franklin's hypocritical and pleasure-destroying materialism—poor Richards can't sleep for fear that he won't remember the good deed he has done to Goodson (he has done none) which has put him in such a favorable light with the mysterious stranger. "His imagination-mill was hard at work," Clemens remarks, and there is a brilliant section of the story on the endless processes of human rationalization. And then Richards suddenly realizes what the good deed was! Goodson had been engaged to a very sweet and pretty girl named Nancy Hewitt; the match had been broken off, and the girl had died:

Soon after the girl's death the village found out, or thought it had found out, that she carried a spoonful of negro blood in her veins. Richards worked at these details a good while . . .[and] he seemed to dimly remember that it was *he* that found out about the negro blood; that it was he that told the village; that the village told Goodson where they got it; that he thus saved Goodson from marrying the tainted girl; that he had done him this great service without knowing that he *was* doing it; but that Goodson knew the value of it, and what a narrow escape he had had, and so went to his grave grateful to his benefactor and wishing he had a fortune to leave him.

What a remarkable "inversion" of truth has Mark Twain wrought here—or perhaps what a horrifying statement of truth as it appears to poor Richards. What a nice intuition it was to bring the race question into this parable of financial corruption in the new American Empire—as the small towns of the western frontier also fell under the spell of the great American fortunes in the vast sea change of the Old Republic toward the end of the nineteenth century.

Just as the literary techniques of "Hadleyburg Corrupted" move from the psychological core of the story—the brilliant rationalizing of highly discreditable behavior—to a social scene of general corruption, so Clemens himself was now projecting the psychological tensions of his own financial crisis into the social and historical scene around him. So all art moves from the specific to the universal; and what is important to note, of course, is not only the foolish behavior of Clemens himself during the whole period of his financial speculations, but the rich rewards which he reaped in his writing. His bankruptcy was not his undoing, as might have happened with a lesser talent, and as some Mark Twain critics have maintained about him—it was instead a kind of spiritual death and rebirth. What mattered in the end, as I say, was not so much his own suffering during this whole period as the new artistic purpose formed by his suffering; and he was to endure, and, yes, *use,* in the highest artistic sense, even to the last ordeal of his domestic tragedy.

One notices, also, in the central figures of "The Man That Corrupted Hadleyburg," not only the constant attempt to deceive others, but far worse, the continuous and unconscious process of *self-deception.* When Richards has finally reached the "solution" of the service he had done Goodson—the matter of the Negro blood in the "tainted girl"—his spirit is completely at peace. "It was all clear and simple now, and the more he went over it the more luminous and certain it grew; and at last, when he nestled to sleep satisfied and happy, he remembered the whole thing just as if it had been yesterday. In fact, he dimly remembered Goodson's *telling* him his gratitude once. Meantime Mary had spent six thousand dollars on a new house for herself and a pair of slippers for her pastor, and then had fallen peacefully to rest."

The whole community indulges in a spree of imaginary spending. The new architect in "this unpromising town" finds himself deluged by secret plans for palatial new houses. "The days drifted along, and the bill of future squanderings rose higher and higher, wilder and wilder, more and more foolish and reckless. It began to look as if every member of the "Nineteen" would not only spend his whole forty thousand dollars before receiving-day, but be actually in debt by the time he got the money. In some cases light-headed people did not stop with planning to spend, they really spent—on credit." And while Sam Clemens knew this from deep personal experience, he was also anticipating a whole new epoch of credit-financing and installment-buying on which a later American economy would come to rest—perhaps to thrive.

Hadleyburg was another early example of Thorstein Veblen's conspicuous consumption. What we see here is the disintegration of the whole town's structure, social and personal relationships alike, under the lure and pressure of an "imaginary fortune." While those great fortunes of Clemens' own period which were real did even more harm to the social patterns and moral values of the Old Republic than the symbolic one in Mark Twain's story. Clemens was also describing, in the chronicle of a disintegrating Hannibal—which became Hadleyburg, which became hell—the cultural impact of the titans and the trusts; of the new social-economic regime of monopoly capitalism in the United States. The rest of the mysterious message, which was *not* given to any of the aspiring "Nineteeners" in the town, read: "Go, and reform—or, mark my words—some day, for your sins, you will die and go to hell or Hadleyburg—*try and make it the former.*"

STANLEY BRODWIN
MARK TWAIN'S MASK OF SATAN IN 'HADLEYBURG'

"The Man That Corrupted Hadleyburg" embodies Twain's cynicism concerning the damned human race in the character of the vengeful stranger. In this Western version of the fall, the lines of action are determined, both artistically and philosophically, by Satan—or Howard L. Stephenson, as he is called.

Exerpted from "Mark Twain's Masks of Satan: The Final Phase," *American Literature,* 45 (May 1973), 208–212. Copyright © 1973 by Duke University Press. Reprinted by permission of Duke University Press (title is editor's).

Stephenson, a "ruined gambler" (p. 353), begins the action of the story by translating his anger at Hadleyburg into a plan for corrupting it. "Bitter" and "revengeful" (p. 352), he is actually as guilty of spiritual pride as his victims. In the mythical ramification of the biblical story, Satan also falls through pride and is thereby able to recognize and penetrate to the pride in Adam and Eve. Stephenson does indeed expose an inherently sinful Hadleyburg. His last "gamble" pays off. Critics have therefore read the tale as Mark Twain's "affirmation" of his belief in man's ability to learn and accept the truth about himself. From that point of view, Satan's role is easily interpreted as that of a "savior." But the many complex ironies in the story suggest another interpretation. Satan-Stephenson, as in the traditional Christian view, wins only to lose, since at the end he is duped into thinking Richards was in fact incorruptible. At the same time, the ending of the story in which we find the citizens of Hadleyburg willing to confront temptation and not be caught "napping" (p. 343) again, does not necessarily suggest any real *moral* change in them that would justify reading the conclusion as a genuine version of the *felix culpa*. We can see this by examining the complex and ironic relationships Stephenson triggers, but which entrap him, too.

One of the most piercing ironies in the story derives from the relationship between Edward Richards and Burgess, a relationship Stephenson exploits after Mary and Edward discover the sack of "gold" (actually lead discs) left by Stephenson. Their initial response is to keep it and to burn the note which orders the money to go to the man who gave advice to Stephenson, whose exact words are recorded in a sealed envelope. Mary and Edward momentarily control themselves and assume that the advice was given by Barclay Goodson, the good samaritan, now dead. Of course, Goodson had not been brought up in Hadleyburg. They then wonder why the stranger made the hated Burgess the one to deliver the wealth, and they discuss the fact that Edward was guilty of not clearing Burgess from some (unnamed) accusation which destroyed his reputation. The implication, as the story progresses, is that Stephenson somehow knows this, but counts on Burgess's repaying Edward with kindness. This Burgess does, for in the grand revelation scene in which he reveals the letters of eighteen of the town's "incorruptible" families, he holds back Edward's note containing the secret advice: "You are far from being a bad man: Go, and reform" (p. 365). By preventing the Richardses' disgrace, Burgess unwittingly exposes them to a second temptation. They accept the proceeds from the sack the town had auctioned off. But our elderly Adam and Eve are destroyed by guilt, for they become obsessed with the idea that Burgess was kind only to expose them later in revenge for Richards's earlier failure to help him. Although Richards had warned

Burgess to leave town so as to avoid being tarred and feathered, he did not clear him. The dying Richards therefore convinces himself that Burgess "repented of the saving kindness which he had done me, and he *exposed* me" (p. 392). But Burgess had not exposed the Richardses, and is ironically hurt by them again. He will be more hated than ever now. Stephenson's plan succeeds because he has insight into both the weaknesses and the strengths of his victims. He is, so to speak, a *psychological* determinist, capable of creating a situation in which people can be emotionally manipulated toward his desired end: mutual physical or spiritual destruction. This Satan has insight into *guilt,* just as, in "The Mysterious Stranger" fables, "44" can read minds. Stephenson emerges, in part, as a demonic mask for Mark Twain's own obsession with guilt, turned here to destructive rather than creative purposes. One of the consequences of such power, however, is to risk exile, a frequent condition for many of Twain's characters other than Satan. In "Hadleyburg," Twain gives us Burgess and Halliday, perhaps as pointed contrasts to Stephenson, for they are both good men who have grown embittered in their social exile.

Halliday is described as "the loafing, good-natured, no-account, irreverent fisherman, hunter, boys' friend, stray-dogs' friend, typical 'Sam Lawson' of the town" (p. 362). He also becomes, in part, the author's satiric voice, a grown-up Huck Finn. The change in the people is not noticed "except by Jack Halliday, who always noticed everything; and always made fun of it, too, no matter what it was" (p. 363). Here we see an Adamic figure developing a "Satanic" characteristic, that inability to believe in the essential goodness of others. If he exists at all, the "good" man is pushed towards exile, with its embitterment and estrangement. However unwilling, man may come to share a common vision with his Arch-Enemy. "The Mysterious Stranger" stories may be read as a demonstration of this idea, as well.

It is given to the Richardses to recognize the larger tragic dimension of the situation Stephenson created. Confronting his lie-filled life, Edward realizes that the money "came from Satan. I saw the hell-brand on them, and I knew they were sent to betray me to sin" (p. 391). And again: "like the rest I fell when temptation came" (p. 392). Still, this confession, however "realistic" and "affirmative" it may be, serves only to create yet another lie: that Burgess had exposed him. To the end, Richards is trapped in lies, whether motivated by greed or by what he felt was the truth of man's nature.

Mary, too, has her insight. When Edward rationalizes that it "was so ordered" (p. 360) that the money be sent to them, she replies:

Ordered! Oh, everything's *ordered*, when a person has to find some way out when he has been stupid. Just the same, it was *ordered* that the money should come to us in this special way, and it was you that must take it on yourself to go meddling with the designs of Providence—and who gave you the right? It was wicked, that is what it was—just blasphemous presumption.

Her point is clear, and reflects Mark Twain's own view of the matter. Man invokes Destiny or a form of determinism to bolster his own selfish rationalizations. The next step is to meddle with Providence. For what *is* ordered is man's pride which leads him to destined ends in spite of himself. The revised motto of Hadleyburg, "Lead Us Into Temptation" (p. 393), is not merely a recognition that morality must be continually tested by experience, though of course that is an important theme in the fable. The deeper meaning seems to be that the only way to confront destiny is to surrender to it. At least man will not be caught "napping" when he falls, but fall he must. But the grand irony is that Satan will not see the proof of this. He, too, is a victim of the lie, and writes to Richards that he is *"a disappointed man. Your honesty is beyond the reach of temptation"* (p. 389). This appears so only because, as the reader knows, Burgess did not tell the truth at the court. Satan is justified in thinking that all men will fall when tempted, but the reality of it eludes him. Also eluding him will be the consolation that Hadleyburg has not really changed. Certainly, Hadleyburg will be shrewder, more careful, more alert, in the future. The citizens welcome temptation, not because any profound moral change has taken place in them, but because they are now "experienced." Twain's implication, I believe, is that expediency will still be the basis of morality, a conviction he often expressed throughout his writings. To be sure, a morality based on "enlightened" expediency is better than the sham, self-righteous attitudes of the Hadleyburgians before the fall, and must not be despised. But it is not authentic moral reform. One thinks of an early Twain quip: "the serene confidence which a Christian feels with four aces." No doubt Stephenson, the ruined gambler, would have bitterly recognized the truth of that description.

7

THE $30,000 BEQUEST

Written in 1903 in Florence where the family had retired in vain hope of improving Olivia Clemens' health, "The $30,000 Bequest" was published in *Harper's Weekly*, Dec. 10, 1904. The story was also featured in the collection *The $30,000 Bequest and Other Stories.*

The lure of money in this tale is similar to the snare that enticed Twain's father into illusive hopes for realizing a fortune from a vast tract of inherited land in Tennessee. Twain writes in his *Autobiography* about the family's frustrated dreams of wealth:

It [the Tennessee land] kept us hoping and hoping during forty years and forsook us at last. It put our energies to sleep and made visionaries out of all of us—dreamers and indolent. . . . It is good to begin life poor; it is good to begin life rich—these are wholesome; but to begin it poor and *prospectively* rich! The man who has not experienced it cannot imagine the curse of it.

It is not, of course, money *per se* which undermines human happiness but rather the preoccupation with money which distorts its importance. Twain saw his celebrated contemporary, Commodore Vanderbilt, as the epitome of this acquisitive impulse that infused society during the Gilded Age. "Poor Vanderbilt!" Twain wrote,

How I do pity you; and this is honest. You are an old man, and ought to have some rest, and yet you have to struggle and struggle, and deny yourself, and rob yourself of restful sleep and peace of mind because you need money so badly. I always feel for a man as poverty ridden as you. Don't misunderstand me, Vanderbilt. I know you own seventy millions; but then you know and I know that it isn't what a man has that constitutes wealth. No—it is to be satisfied with what one has: that is wealth.

(Quoted by Philip Foner)

"The $30,000 Bequest" is Twain's artistic delineation of the insidious consequences of the acquisitive values which were then and still are embodied in the American Dream.

MAXWELL GEISMAR
TWAIN'S PARODY OF SMALL SOULS ON THE MAKE

"The $30,000 Bequest" was a kind of sequel to "The Man That Corrupted Hadleyburg," as another example of what money and greed can do to the human psyche; another fable of the cultural damage wrought by the epoch of the great fortunes upon the agrarian-mercantile simplicity of the Old Republic. Saladin Foster is a bookkeeper in the Far West town of Lakeside; his wife Electra is a capable helpmate who has done some minor speculations in real estate from their frugal life and modest savings. (Saladin is called Sally, Electra Aleck, in a curious sexual transposition of Clemens' in this dream and nightmare tale.) Their two daughters are Clytemnestra and Gwendolyn; they are a loving, affectionate, virtuous family—until the fraudulent promise of wealth ruins them all.

From a distant relative, Tilbury Foster, they learn they are to receive some thirty thousand dollars cash "not for love, but because money had given him most of his troubles and exasperations, and he wished to place it where there was good hope that it would continue its malignant work." And provided that the Fosters could prove to the executors of the estate that they had never taken any notice of this gift, had made no inquiries about "the moribund's progress toward the everlasting tropics," and had not attended the funeral, etc. Now the story's scene is set, and once again Clemens was projecting his own gambling fever and financial follies into his art and his society alike.

The ordeal of the Fosters begins; their whole obscure, commonplace, decent, and affectionate small-town life is corrupted and devalued. But just as Clemens had reversed symbolically the sexual role of these domestic partners, so he reversed their financial roles. It is Aleck who spends her

From *Mark Twain: An American Prophet* by Maxwell Geismar. Copyright © 1970 by Maxwell Geismar. Used by permission of the publisher, Houghton Mifflin Company (title is editor's).

days absorbed in investing this imaginary fortune; while Sally is planning how to spend it. One might say, Freudianly, that Clemens was now shifting his own financial guilt to the dead Livy in part. But it makes more sense to say that the two central characters in the story represent the double personality of Clemens himself: the romantic and naive financial "promoter"; the idle and happy pleasure-lover. Meanwhile the children slip away from these distraught parents who make their first imaginary gamble in cannel-coal mining stocks; the whole tissue of their domestic life together is eroded by their mutual obsession of making and spending their new fortune. (Based on the inheritance which they have not yet received, which we surmise does not exist.) Here indeed Mark Twain was showing how easily our ordinary material life can be controlled by, and made completely and obsessively part of, our dream and fantasy life . . . if indeed our daily material existence *does* exist apart from our psychic existence, in the curious interchange of illusion and reality.

But this tale was part of the whole literary process, as we know the psychologists don't seem to understand, by which Clemens himself was expressing an artistic catharsis of his own earlier panic and frustration in the business world. If he had not suffered through the bankruptcy ordeal, he would not have understood, much less created such literature—in which a deeply personal experience was fused with a very pertinent kind of social criticism. Without the personal experience, the cultural force of these stories would not have been so valid; without the cultural framework of the material change in the older American Republic which Mark Twain both witnessed and described, the personal experience would have been trivial and meaningless. The Fosters soon raise their imaginary capital to imaginary heights; they make a hundred thousand dollars by speculating on margin; they are completely absorbed by their obsession at the expense of children, friends, and homelife, even while they decide to invest (in their fancy) in a luxurious new home, and give a party to celebrate (since they are unable to confide their secret dream of wealth to anybody) the "Discovery of America." Then, of course, no ordinary village suitors are up to the financial-social position of the children whom in fact they have almost rejected as human beings. Starting with a dreamlike fantasy indeed, Clemens makes "The $30,000 Bequest" into a brilliant parody (anticipating a favorite theme of Ring Lardner's) of small American souls on the make; or of the ambitious new financial-social aristocracy which Veblen was describing in similar terms during the same years.

We realize, too, while "Hadleyburg" was a savage and ironical parable of the hypocrisy of human virtue, and the ease of human temptation, that "The $30,000 Bequest" is primarily a comedy on the same theme. The relations between the Fosters are good-humored and affectionate in the depths of their mutual obsession. This is even a tender comedy about poor, weak human nature on the part of the "bitter," the "thwarted," the "frustrated" and "defeated" Mark Twain. There are the imaginary gas bills that Aleck frets about and Sally enjoys. And if there are curious elements of Freudian displacement in this story, one realizes that Clemens was describing one of the worst periods of the domestic abyss with all the grace, affection, humor of the domestic idyll. This is a remarkable re-creation of experience in literary terms whereby the artist was purging himself through the divine release of humor and self-humor. Now indeed the Foster daughters are no longer available in matrimony to the mechanics and shopkeepers of the Old Republic; their wealthy, successful, respectable parents are surveying the lists of lawyers, doctors, and successful financiers.

The Fosters themselves take on a new dignity and gravity of deportment as befitting superior souls who have become persons of property—substantial property. They have now accumulated half a million dollars—a million—and they exhibit, said Clemens, "the pride of riches." Mansion succeeds mansion in their dream life; they finally select Newport, Rhode Island, "Holy Land of High Society, ineffable Domain of the American aristocracy" . . . As a rule they spent a part of every Sabbath—after morning service—in this sumptuous home, the rest of it they spent in Europe, or in dawdling around in their private yacht. And then: "Aleck, in her dream life, went over to the Episcopal camp, on account of its large official titles; next she became High-church on account of the candles and shows; and next she naturally changed to Rome, where there were cardinals and more candles."

Veblenian accents indeed of conspicuous consumption and ostentatious display, and the whole modern drift of American society. And then comes the passage of Sally-Sam's burlesque "confession" after he has accused Aleck of shipping off her missionaries "to persuade unreflecting Chinamen to trade off twenty-four carat Confucianism for counterfeit Christianity." Aleck bursts into tears at his teasing and the spectacle breaks Sally's heart and leads him to tremendous self-accusation. "His cheeks burned and his soul was steeped in humiliation. Look at her life—how fair it was, and tending ever upward; and look at his own—how frivolous, how charged with mean vanities, how selfish, how empty, how ignoble! And its trend—never upward, but downward, ever downward!"

He instituted comparisons between her record and his own. He had found fault with her—so he mused—*he!* And what could he say for himself? When she built her first church, what was he doing? Gathering other blasé millionaires into a Poker Club; defiling his own palace with it; losing hundreds of thousands to it at every sitting, and sillily vain of the admiring notoriety it made for him. When she was building her first university, what was he doing? Polluting himself with a gay and dissipated secret life in the company of other fast bloods, multi-millionaires in money and paupers in character. When she was building her first foundling asylum, what was he doing? Alas! When she was projecting her noble Society for the Purifying of the Sex, what was he doing? Ah, what, indeed! When she and the W.C.T.U. and the Woman with the Hatchet, moving with resistless march, were sweeping the fatal bottle from the land, what was he doing? Getting drunk three times a day. When she, builder of a hundred cathedrals, was being gratefully welcomed and blest in papal Rome and decorated with the Golden Rose which she had so honorably earned, what was he doing? Breaking the bank at Monte Carlo.

And so much, you might say, for those Mark Twain critics, and perhaps primarily Messrs. Kaplan and Fiedler and their Freudian cohorts who continually stress the burden of Samuel Clemens' "guilt" in his relations with Livy and the children. For Clemens himself in his best moments completely dissipated the whole psychological syndrome of "guilt-anxiety-shame-and-self-punishment" which might apply to ordinary mortals. At the worst moment of his defeat and despair—the moment of Livy's final fatal illness—he could yet sieze upon the liberation of art which was based upon self-insight, affection, and humor. How Clemens, in "The $30,000 Bequest," satirized both himself and Livy while projecting their private torment outward into a comic fable of human greed. How the incorrigible and finally *unrepentant* spirit that was Mark Twain, this demonic and diabolical angel of our literature—this mad scoundrel, if you like, of whose compulsions and contradictions great art was made—always pushed things one step *more!* And thus to redeem and reclaim and indeed to end up celebrating all his human failings under the light of his literary grace. In the same story, moreover, Clemens concluded by a sweet and touching parody of his lifelong "confessions" of sin to Livy. The "guilty" hero decides he must tell all to his wife and financial mate:

He stopped. He could go no farther; he could not bear the rest. He rose up, with a great resolution upon his lips: this secret life should be revealed, and confessed; no longer could he live it clandestinely; he would go and tell her All.

And that is what he did. He told her All; and wept upon her bosom; wept and moaned, and begged for her forgiveness. It was a profound shock, and she staggered under the blow, but he was her own, the core of her heart, the blessing of her eyes, her all in all, she could deny him nothing, and she forgave him. She felt that he could never again be quite to her what he had been before; she knew that he could only repent and not reform; yet all morally defaced and decayed as he was, was he not her own, her very own, the idol of her deathless worship? She said she was his serf, his slave, and she opened her yearning heart and took him in.

Touching lines indeed; but was Sam taking liberties with Livy's true feelings about him, her true vision of their bond? Maybe so, but this theme is repeated so steadily in the writings both during and after Livy's death, and with such confidence, affection, and beneficent humor, that we must really assume that Samuel Clemens knew more about his own private life than some of the later, and more skeptical critics. And the final record, in any case, is always in a writer's art rather than in his "other"—that is to say his private, personal, and much less important—life.

The ending of "The $30,000 Bequest," like so many of Mark Twain's endings, was lurid and heavy, as the Fosters receive the news that they have been tricked by a malicious relative who had no fortune to bequeath; and like the "honest" couple in "The Man That Corrupted Hadleyburg," they lose their sanity. (The symbolic moral of the story, however, is quite accurate; and Sally does finally reflect, at the peak of his insanity, that the whole trouble was that Tilbury Foster should have left them *more* money.)

GERALD J. FENGER
THE COMPLEX IRONY OF "THE $30,000 BEQUEST"

In 1904, five years after "Hadleyburg," Twain published another rather long short story, "The $30,000 Bequest." This twenty-five page yarn (divided into eight sections) has much the same theme as Hadleyburg: "Bequest" details the destructive effect of obsessive, all-consuming greed upon a man and his wife. The couple could easily have been modelled upon the Richardses in "Hadleyburg," at least the Richardses could have served as an inspiration, a starting point for the "Bequest" pair.

. . . a pleasant little town of five or six thousand inhabitants, and a rather pretty one, too, as towns go in the Far West. It had church accommodations for 35,000, which is the way of the Far West and the South, where everybody is religious, and where each of the Protestant sects is represented and has a plant of its own (500).

From an unpublished dissertation, *Perspectives of Satire in Mark Twain's Short Stories* (Texas Christian University, 1974), pp. 243–253. Used by permission of the author (title is editor's).

By pointing out the surplus of church pews and referring to the various churches as "plants," Twain is obviously poking fun at fundamentalist, "Bible-belt" religion found in the West and South. The whole story is an attack upon two "super-pious" people who are too ignorant of themselves to recognize their complete and utter materialism and their lack of any true spiritual values whatsoever.

As the story opens the reader is introduced to the two main characters, Saladin and Electra Foster, and he observes that the omniscient speaker will relate the chronicle of the Fosters in retrospective fashion. Saladin was the "book-keeper in the principal store, and the only high-salaried man of his profession in Lakeside" (500). His wife, Electra, was "a private dabbler in romance" (500) who had made money on real estate transactions in their first fourteen years of marriage and who had an independent income from her investments in property. Her aggressive, masculine personality traits fit well with her nickname, Aleck. Her husband's obviously submissive character also fits well, in turn, with his feminine nickname, Sally. There appears to be an imminent danger in this reversal of traditional family roles, and the feeling of trouble looming for the Fosters is strengthened by the knowledge that the family, including the two daughters, Clytemnestra and Gwendolyn, read romances to each other. We know that in Twain's view anyone who reads and enjoys romances is simply asking for trouble.

And trouble comes, though it is not recognized as such until it is too late. The Fosters are nearly overwhelmed with joy when they receive word that a distant relative of Sally's, Tilbury Foster, a seventy-year-old bachelor, is expected to shortly die and leave Sally

thirty thousand dollars cash; not for love, but because money had given him most of his troubles and exasperations, and he wished to place it where there was good hope that it would continue its malignant work. The bequest would be found in his will and would be paid over. *Provided, that Sally should be able to prove to the executors that he had taken no notice of the gift by spoken word or by letter, had made no inquiries concerning the moribund's progress toward the everlasting tropics, and had not attended the funeral* (501–2).

Easily overlooking the sarcasm and the portent of grief, the couple are immediately overcome by greed and begin to plan what they will do with (what they already consider to be) their newly acquired fortune. (Just as the principal citizens of Hadleyburg did.)

Soon they get their first newspaper from Tilbury's town, only to learn with dismay that he is apparently still alive. This elicits a well-placed satiric barb from Twain in the form of a revealing conversation that punctures the hypocrisy of their religion:

Aleck was a Christian from the cradle, and duty and the force of habit required her to go through the motions. She pulled herself together and said, with a pious two-per-cent trade joyousness:

"Let us be humbly thankful that he has been spared; and—"

"Damn his treacherous hide, I wish—"

"Sally! For shame!"

"I don't care!" retorted the angry man. "It's the way *you* feel, and if you weren't so immorally pious you'd be honest and say so."

Aleck said with wounded dignity:

"I do not see how you can say such unkind and unjust things. There is no such thing as immoral piety."

Sally, of course, pierces through the seemingly beautiful veneer of religion that his wife possesses and exposes the essential hollowness and rottenness of it at the core; her religion is one of mere forms and conventions—a mechanical following of outward practices with no genuine feeling at all at the center. She is the type of the "Sunday Christian," the person who rarely, if ever, misses church on Sunday, but who immediately upon leaving the church becomes her mean, vicious, conniving, materialistic, greedy, selfish, true self for the rest of the week—the person whose piety is so grossly false as to be truly the essence of immorality.

Cousin Tilbury dies on "schedule," but by an accident, his death notice is left out of the paper, and the Fosters go on waiting. But Aleck wastes no time. She spends the $30,000 in her imagination, and before long she has made $100,000 in imaginary money. The Fosters naturally wish to celebrate their increase in prospectus wealth, but they must keep the real cause a secret, so they celebrate the discovery of America. Their imagined wealth becomes confused with their actual wealth, and in a short time they cannot tell them apart, a phenomenon which prompts the omniscient speaker to remark upon a danger to all men, a danger which Twain had come to know by first-hand experience:

The castle-building habit, the day-dreaming habit—how it grows! What a luxury it becomes; how we fly to its enchantments at every idle moment, how we revel in them, steep our souls in them, intoxicate ourselves with their beguiling fantasies—oh, yes, and how soon and how easily our dream life and our material life become so intermingled and so fused together that we can't quite tell which is which, anymore (510).

So the Fosters begin life in a dream world. Aleck subscribes to financial newspapers and studies them as diligently during the week as she studies her Bible on Sundays. Their "fortune" increases daily, and it is not long before they are reckoning the "fictitious finances" in the millions of dollars. When the sum reaches 2400 million, they know that a crisis point has been reached, for their "holdings" have become so large that it is imperative that they take stock and straighten out their business affairs. They know that to do the job properly and perfectly it must be completed when once it is begun, but where can *they* find the necessary unbroken ten-hour time span necessary to fulfill the task? Sally is busy at the store all day and every day; Aleck is busy doing housework all day and every day; and the daughters, Gwendolyn and Clytemnestra, cannot help for they are being "saved up" for high society. There is only one free ten hour stretch open to them; and so they fall, fall and *break the Sabbath!* They must work on Sunday. The omniscient speaker notes: "It was but another step in the downward path. Others would follow. Vast wealth has temptations which fatally and surely undermine the moral structure of persons not habituated to its possession" (515).

Their holdings (which are "good things, gilt-edged, and interest bearing") are themselves a satire of the stock market, for they include such things as "Diluted Telegraph," "Tammany Graft," and "Shady Privileges in the Post-Office Department" (515). Having found their holdings to be producing an income of $120,000,000 a year, the Fosters decide to "stand pat," retire from "business," and live off the "income." Then, to help keep up with expenses in their sternly restricted fact life, Sally starts to steal from the store where he works: "How easy it is to go from bad to worse when once we have started upon a downward course!" (516). Their "wealth" secure, the Fosters are now free to spend, spend, spend in their one day a week in "Fairyland," a situation which gives Twain an opportunity to fire a few more shots at orthodox religion and its ties with "the root of all evil" and its ostentation:

Aleck, in her dream life, went over to the Episcopal camp, on account of its large official titles; next she became High-church on account of the candles and shows; and next she naturally changed to Rome, where there were more cardinals and more candles. But these excursions were as nothing to Sally's. . . . He worked his religions hard and changed them with his shirt (517).

But religion is not the only sufferer; anything is fair game for attack in Twain's tales, and shortly after he finishes firing at religion, he gives a good-natured punch to "the awful German language." Aleck and Sally's dream life carries them to the point of arranging an imaginary marriage for one of their daughters. Twain makes mincemeat (or should one say sausage?) out of the would-be-groom's title: "His Royal Highness Sigismund-Siegfried-Lauenfeld-Dinkelspiel-Schwartzenberg Blutwurst, Hereditary Grand Duke of Katzenyammer." The marriage to this burlesque Duke never takes place, however, for the fantasy fortune falls victim to a devastating stock-market crash, and the Fosters lose everything.

Only then does the hapless couple come back fully to reality, as Sally suddenly realizes that they "really never invested a penny" of his relative's bequest, "but only its unmaterialized future." They still had the "thirty thousand untouched" (523). Just then the Fosters are interrupted by the editor and proprietor of the *Sagamore*, the local paper in Tilbury Foster's hometown, who is in Lakeside on other business and decides to drop in on the Fosters and collect the money owed on their subscription to his paper for the past four years. In the course of the conversation, Aleck and Sally learn that Tilbury Foster had died five years ago and was penniless; the town even had to pay the cost of his burial. Their minds snap at this revelation, but they live "yet two years, in mental night, always brooding, steeped in vague regrets and melancholy dreams, never speaking"; then release comes "to both on the same day" (525). Shortly before he dies, the darkness lifts from Sally's ruined mind for a moment, and he utters what has to be construed the "moral" of the tale:

"Vast wealth, acquired by sudden and unwholesome means, is a snare. It did us no good, transient were its feverish pleasures; yet for its sake we threw away our sweet and simple and happy life—let others take warning by us" (525).

But Twain's propensity to hit his reader on the head with the superfluous moral tag and, in effect, insult his intelligence is somewhat mitigated in this fine tale, by the inclusion of Sally's last words. Sally, in all-too-human fashion, tried to place the blame for his own errors on someone else; even in dying he tries to "pass the buck" to Tilbury:

"Money had brought him misery, and he took his revenge upon us, who had done him no harm. He had his desire: with base and cunning calculation he left us but thirty thousand, knowing we would try to increase it, and ruin our life and break our hearts. Without added expense he could have left us far above desire of increase, far above the temptation to speculate, and a kinder soul would have done it; but in him was no generous spirit, no pity, no—" (525).

Thus, the story ends on a definitely ironic note. Tilbury could never have "left" the Fosters enough to put them "far above the desire of increase"; their rapacious greed would have inevitably spurred them on to make more. So it is with too many of us in this latter half of the twentieth century "Gilded Age." So it has always been. Twain, continually striving to be a part of the millionaire society of his friend Andrew Carnegie, understood this all too well.

The omniscient speaker in this tale delivers an endless stream of commentary throughout the story, and he delivers it with a great amount of enthusiasm and gusto. This was the last satiric short story that Twain published in his lifetime, and he seemed to pour all his vitality into it, just as the shooting star blazes brightly just before it goes out. The speaker, for example, tells us of the impending death of Tilbury Foster with tremendous verve: "Now came great news! Stunning news—joyous news, in fact!" (501). The speaker frequently probes the minds of the principal characters and often evaluates or judges what he finds there. He describes Sally's feelings after Sally had made a sarcastic remark to his wife, but the speaker also comments on those feelings: "Sally felt a pang, but tried to conceal it under a shuffling attempt to save his case by changing the form of it—as if changing the form while retaining the juice could deceive the expert he was trying to placate" (506). The speaker likewise probes Aleck's mind and evaluates what he finds in her thoughts about Sally: "The dear woman, she knew he had talent; and if affection made her over-estimate the size of it a little, surely it was a sweet and gentle crime, and forgiveable for its source's sake" (512). The narrative voice also enters the minds of both the characters directly by using the first person plural pronoun "we": "If we could have looked out through the eyes of these dreamers, we should have seen their tidy little wooden house disappear, and a two-story brick with a cast-iron fence in front of it take its place" (511).

The omniscient voice moralizes frequently in the story, perhaps almost to the point of over-doing it. He sounds somewhat like Ben Franklin's Poor Richard in *Poor Richard's Almanac*. The speaker constantly hits at his theme about the love of money being the root of all evil and warns his readers: "Vast wealth has temptations which fatally and surely undermine the moral structure of persons not habituated to its possession" (515). "It is the first wrong steps that count. . . . Vast wealth, to the person unaccustomed to it, is a bane; it eats into the flesh and bone of his morals. . . . How easy it is to go from bad to worse, when once we have started upon a downward course" (516).

Sally eventually comes to realize his own depravity, in what amounts to a long probe into his thoughts, and he confesses to Aleck. (Sally becomes fat and bloated, drinks constantly, and, of course, steals from the store where he is employed.) He confesses that in his mind he has become even more licentious, a veritable playboy, and he realizes that he has been constantly attacking her religious beliefs and her pious acts of brotherly love. Twain could have been chastizing himself a bit here, for we know that he continually eroded his wife's once-strong faith.

"The $30,000 Bequest" comes across as a representation of, or a logical extension of, what could happen to the great-expectation dreaming as done in Hadleyburg, if such fantasy were carried to the extreme. The story afforded Twain perhaps one of his best opportunities to use what is called limited or selective omniscience, but he shunned the central consciousness perspective as employed so frequently and so masterfully by his contemporary, Henry James. In fact, Twain did not use the central consciousness point-of-view in any of his short satiric tales, nor in any of his other fiction that I am aware of. The omniscient voice, however, in "$30,000 Bequest" is continually reminding the reader of the presence of a story-teller, and for some readers, this frequent reminder may tend to destroy the illusion of reality that the story attempts to create. The omniscient viewpoint, whenever it is used, offers constant danger that the author may come between the reader and the story, and Twain perhaps pushes this danger to its limits in "Bequest." The reader cannot help making a strong identification of the omniscient speaker with Mark Twain himself. In this story the implied author, or the speaker, and the actual author seem to be one.

8

CAPTAIN STORMFIELD'S
VISIT TO HEAVEN

The story entitled "Extracts from Captain Stormfield's Visit to Heaven," published in the December 1907 and January 1908 issues of *Harper's Magazine,* was written almost forty years earlier (probably in 1868) during Twain's happier days. He thought the satire on religion so scathing that he kept the story, quite literally, locked away in a safe. He had, though, read it to William Dean Howells, and Paine reports that in the winter of 1878 Howells suggested publishing it in England where, presumably, the intellectual climate was less restrictive. But Twain was loath to chance offending his reading public, at home or abroad. So the story languished. Occasionally Twain would take it out, revise it a bit, and stash it away again. He eventually published only a portion of the manuscript.

When "Extracts from Captain Stormfield's Visit to Heaven" finally saw print, no one declared it blasphemous. Indeed, according to Paine, many admirers wrote to express "enjoyment and approval," pleased that Twain had resumed his earlier, light-hearted manner. Today the tale seems extremely mild to have once warranted such caution. While the satirical stabs at Christian hypocrisy and religious orthodoxy are no longer stinging, the humor and charm remain fresh. The story is one of Twain's best.

In the first selection in this section, Mark Twain tells about the real Captain Stormfield, whose name was Captain Ned Wakeman. In the last selection, William M. Gibson explains in admirable detail the background of the story.

S. L. CLEMENS
THE LITERARY EVOLUTION OF
CAPTAIN NED WAKEMAN

I first knew Capt. Wakeman thirty-nine years ago. I made two voyages with him and we became fast friends. He was a great burly, handsome, weather-beaten, symmetrically built and powerful creature, with coal-black hair and whiskers and the kind of eye which men obey without talking back. He was full of human nature, and the best kind of human nature. He was as hearty and sympathetic and loyal and loving a soul as I have found anywhere and when his temper was up he performed all the functions of an earthquake, without the noise.

He was all sailor from head to heel; and this was proper enough, for he was born at sea. In the course of his sixty-five years he had visited the edges of all the continents and archipelagoes, but had never been on land except incidentally and spasmodically, as you may say. He had never had a day's schooling in his life but had picked up worlds and worlds of knowledge at secondhand and none of it correct. He was a liberal talker and inexhaustibly interesting. In the matter of a wide and catholic profanity he had not his peer on the planet while he lived. It was a deep pleasure to me to hear him do his stunts in this line. He knew the Bible by heart and was profoundly and sincerely religious. He was always studying the Bible when it was his watch below and always finding new things, fresh things and unexpected delights and surprises in it—and he loved to talk about his discoveries and expound them to the ignorant. He believed that he was the only man on the globe that really knew the secret of the Biblical miracles. He had what he believed was a sane and rational explanation of every one of them and he loved to teach his learning to the less fortunate.

I have said a good deal about him in my books. In one of them I have told how he brought the murderer of his colored mate to trial in the Chincha Islands before the assembled captains of the ships in port, and how when sentence had been passed he drew the line there. He had intended to capture and execute the murderer all by himself but had been persuaded by the captains to let them try him with the due formalities

From *The Autobiography of Mark Twain,* ed. Charles Neider (New York: Harper & Bros., 1959), pp. 275-278. Copyright © 1959 by The Mark Twain Company. Copyright 1959 by Charles Neider. Reprinted by permission of Harper & Row, Inc. (title is editor's).

and under the forms of law. He had yielded that much, though most reluctantly, but when the captains proposed to do the executing also, that was too much for Wakeman and he struck. He hanged the man himself. He put the noose around the murderer's neck, threw the bight of the line over the limb of a tree, and made his last moments a misery to him by reading him nearly into premature death with random and irrelevant chapters from the Bible.

He was a most winning and delightful creature. When he was fifty-three years old he started from a New England port, master of a great clipper ship bound around the Horn for San Francisco, and he was not aware that he had a passenger but he was mistaken as to that. He had never had a love passage but he was to have one now. When he was out from port a few weeks he was prowling about some remote corner of his ship, by way of inspection, when he came across a beautiful girl, twenty-five years old, prettily clothed and lying asleep with one plump arm under her neck. He stopped in his tracks and stood and gazed, enchanted. Then he said, "It's an angel—that's what it is. It's an angel. When it opens its eyes if they are blue I'll marry it."

The eyes turned out to be blue and the pair were married when they reached San Francsico. The girl was to have taught school there. She had her appointment in her pocket—but the Captain saw to it that that arrangement did not materialize. He built a little house in Oakland—ostensibly a house, but really it was a ship, and had all a ship's appointments, binnacle, scuppers and everything else—and there he and his little wife lived an ideal life during the intervals that intervened between his voyages. They were a devoted pair and worshiped each other. By and by there were two little girls and then the nautical paradise was complete.

Captain Wakeman had a fine large imagination and he once told me of a visit which he had made to heaven. I kept it in my mind and a month or two later I put it on paper—this was in the first quarter of 1868, I think. It made a small book of about forty thousand words and I called it *Captain Stormfield's Visit to Heaven*. Five or six years afterward I showed the manuscript to Howells and he said, "Publish it."

But I didn't. I had turned it into a burlesque of *The Gates Ajar,* a book which had imagined a mean little ten-cent heaven about the size of Rhode Island—a heaven large enough to accommodate about a tenth of one per cent of the Christian billions who had died in the past nineteen centuries. I raised the limit; I built a properly and rationally stupendous heaven and augmented its Christian population to ten per cent of the contents of the modern cemeteries; also, as a volunteer kindness I let in a tenth of one percent of the pagans who had died during the preceding eons—a liberty which was not justifiable because those people had no business there, but as I had merely done it in pity and out of kindness I allowed them to stay. Toward the end of the book my heaven grew to such inconceivable dimensions on my hands that I ceased to apply poor little million-mile measurements to its mighty territories and measured them by light-years only! and not only that, but a million of them linked together in a stretch.

In the thirty-eight years which have since elapsed I have taken out that rusty old manuscript several times and examined it with the idea of printing it, but I always concluded to let it rest. However, I mean to put it into this autobiography now. It is not likely to see the light for fifty years yet, and at that time I shall have been so long under the sod that I shan't care about the results.

I used to talk to [the Rev. Mr. Joseph] Twichell about Wakeman, there in Hartford thirty years ago and more, and by and by a curious thing happened. Twichell went off on a vacation and as usual he followed his vacation custom, that is to say he traveled under an alias so that he could associate with all kinds of disreputable characters and have a good time and nobody be embarassed by his presence, since they wouldn't know that he was a clergyman. He took a Pacific mail ship and started south for the Isthmus. Passenger traffic in that line had ceased almost entirely. Twichell found but one other passenger on board. He noticed that that other passenger was not a saint, so he went to fore-gathering with him at once, of course. After that passenger had delivered himself of about six majestically and picturesquely profane remarks Twichell (alias Peters) said, "Could it be, by chance, that you are Captain Ned Wakeman of San Francisco?"

His guess was right and the two men were inseparable during the rest of the voyage. One day Wakeman asked Peters-Twichell if he had ever read the Bible. Twichell said a number of things in reply, things of a rambling and noncommittal character, but, taken in the sum, they left the impression that Twichell—well, never mind the impression; suffice it that Wakeman set himself the task of persuading Twichell to read that book. He also set himself the task of teaching Twichell how to understand the miracles. He expounded to him, among other miracles, the adventure of Isaac with the prophets of Baal. Twichell could have told him that it wasn't Isaac, but that wasn't Twichell's game and he didn't make the correction. It was a delicious story and it is delightful to hear Twichell tell it. I have printed it in full in one of my books—I don't remember which one.

GLADYS BELLAMY
THE NARRATIVE PERFECTION OF "CAPTAIN STORMFIELD'S VISIT TO HEAVEN"

We come now to the more or less neglected story called *Captain Storm-field's Visit to Heaven,* published in 1908. According to Paine, Mark Twain began the story in 1868 and worked on it intermittently for forty years. It is foreshadowed, however, in a Western sketch of 1863, devoted to Mark Twain's adventures among the spiritualists; he questions one of the "irrepressible Smiths" resident in the spirit world about life in the here-after. According to this particular Smith,

there are spheres—grades of perfection—he is making pretty good prog-ress—has been promoted a sphere or so . . . he don't know how many spheres there are (but I suppose there must be millions, because if a man goes galloping through them at the rate this old Universalist is doing, he will get through an infinitude of them . . . I am afraid the old man is scouring along rather too fast . . .) . . . . I sincerely hope he will continue to progress . . . until he lands on the roof of the highest sphere of all.

In 1878 when Orion Clemens was attempting to write a visit to hell, burlesquing Jules Verne, he had appealed to Mark Twain for literary advice. Mark Twain suggested some of the technical difficulties and gave warning that Orion was "not advanced enough in literature to venture upon a matter" so precarious:

Nine years ago I mapped out my "Journey to Heaven." . . . I gave it a deal of thought. . . . After a year or more I wrote it up. It was not a success. Five years ago I wrote it again . . . but still it wouldn't do. . . . So I thought and thought . . . and at last I struck what I considered to be the right plan! Mind, I have never altered the *ideas* . . . the plan was the difficulty. Now . . . I have tried, all these years, to think of some way of "doing" hell too—and have always had to give it up. Hell, in my book, will not occupy five pages of MS . . . it will be only covert hints.

The plan was to good purpose. This story is, with the exception of *Huckleberry Finn,* Mark Twain's best fictional expression of the two-fold aspect of life. This fact may be accounted for in several ways. He works inside the mind of Captain Stormfield, whose prototype, Captain Ned Wakeman, he described elsewhere (under the name of Hurricane

From *Mark Twain as a Literary Artist,* pp. 368-370. Copyright © 1950 by the Uni-versity of Oklahoma Press, publishing division of the University. Reprinted by permission (title is editor's).

Jones) as "only a gray and bearded child . . . an innocent, lovable old infant." As when he works inside the childlike mind of Nigger Jim, or speaks through the lips of the boy Huck Finn, this childish quality in Stormfield at once operates to give the necessary perspective by removing Mark Twain from him. But perhaps even more effective, here, is the device by which Stormfield looks back on the earth from a point far away in the sky, as if he were looking through a telescope; this device reduces everything to microscopic proportions. Aided by these devices, Mark Twain describes Heaven in a way that makes existence there the well-rounded sort of life he was generally unwilling to accept for life on earth.

When Captain Stormfield arrives at Heaven after "whizzing through space" for thirty years and racing a comet at one point, he announces that he is from the earth. The puzzled clerk, using a great magnifying glass, finally identifies the earth as a speck the heavenly clerical staff commonly call "the Wart." Stormfield demands his personal halo, harp, and wings, and rushes off to a cloud bank to join the heavenly choir. But he finds that singing hymns and waving palm branches is a dull and boresome business, stops singing, and "dumps his cargo": "heaven is . . . just the busiest place you ever heard of. There ain't any idle people here after the first day." Having worked hard, the people have good appetites and sleep well. "It's the same here as it is on earth—you've got to earn a thing, square and honest, before you enjoy it."

Heaven is explained to the Captain by Sandy McWilliams, formerly of New Jersey. Sandy makes it clear that sorrow and disappointment, as well as work, are a part of Heaven, so that happiness becomes the sweeter by reason of the contrast. A woman passes, with tears running down her face. Her baby girl had died years before; and, when she came to Heaven herself, she expected to get her baby back again. But in Heaven one can be whatever age one wishes, and this particular baby has elected to grow up. Moreover, she has improved her mind with "deep scientific learning" until a wide gulf now exists between mother and daughter:

"... what will they do—stay unhappy forever in heaven?"
"No, they'll come together and get adjusted by and by. But not this year, and not next. By and by."

In Heaven, it seems, there is time for the slow amelioration of ills which the impatient Mark Twain could never quite acknowledge on earth. And Heaven need not possess the perfection he seems to have demanded for earthly life. His Heaven shows clearly that pain is necessary for human growth and that both pain and growth are a part of the progress which man continues to make in Heaven.

LOUIS BUDD
TWAIN'S SATIRE ON RACISM

Born to an era of rising nationalism, Twain had steadily fought clear of its excesses and the prejudice that usually came with them. Perhaps the brightest side of his whole intellectual career is his progress away from racism. As he kept refining his vision of Captain Stormfield's great voyage he made room in paradise for everybody—Negroes of course and Chinese, Arabs, Incas, and even white men (who found themselves an obscure minority there). Inside heaven or out he had long since dropped his Washoe tagline that "No Irish need apply." More slowly, the American Indians also stalked into the circle of his sympathy as he became capable of realizing how the pioneer had pre-empted their lands and smashed their culture. Twain's final musings decided that "Patriotism, even at its best—& scarcest—has one blemish—it naturally erects barriers against the B of M—makes that phrase a delicious sarcasm." He could use initials for the brotherhood of man because it was so heavy on his mind that he would not forget what this note meant. Fittingly, he named his last house Stormfield, a token of his bitter struggles to establish the truth but also of an ideal he now held without reservation.

Though economics and politics outgrew Twain's frame of reference, his passion for honesty had led him well. Raised in a sleepy village that was an obsolete social form soon after he left it, he moved far beyond provinciality; mostly self-educated he arrived at better human answers than many savants. As he browsed through every continent and most islands he learned without reading Thoreau that your worst neighbor may be yourself. If he had thought of counting the cats in Zanzibar he would have done it, but if the count came late in his life it would have been uncondescending and fair; having given up dollar diplomacy he would not have twisted his figures into a pretext for a white man's coup. He ended up a true cosmopolitan and an unpaid yet energetic ambassador to any country including his own that would listen. If our spaceships find the sky-blue men with seven heads that Captain Stormfield saw in heaven, we can do much worse than to meet them the way Twain would have done.

From *Mark Twain: Social Philosopher* (Bloomington, Ind.: Indiana University Press, 1962), pp. 189-190. Reprinted by permission of the Indiana University Press (title is editor's).

JAMES M. COX

CAPTAIN STORMFIELD AS PURE BURLESQUE FIGURE

The decisive fact of form in Captain Stormfield's adventure is that it is presented not as a complete work, but as a publishable extract from forbidden materials. The narrative drew upon experiences going all the way back to Mark Twain's San Francisco days, and in Captain Stormfield he presented a figure as irrepressible as Simon Wheeler. In light of their interminable voices, it is not surprising that at one time, early in the nineties, Mark Twain considered replacing Stormfield with the character of Wheeler.

Yet Stormfield is an altogether different figure from Wheeler. Instead of being the deadpan, naively innocent figure who slides effortlessly through his tale, apparently unaware of the comicalities he is disclosing, Stormfield is the all-knowing figure—brash, confident, energetically reckless, and assertive—who speaks a racy slang. Far from standing in apparent confusion at the mercy of his recollection, Stormfield confidently relates his own adventure. He is, in fine, the transcendent stanger full of himself and his journey, moving at a highhanded pace through the revered geography of heaven.

His slang and his fantasy relate his identity not to Huckleberry Finn and Simon Wheeler but to Hank Morgan. Unlike Morgan, however, Stormfield remains a "pure" burlesque figure for two reasons. First of all, by setting the scene in heaven, Mark Twain was able to maintain a balanced inversion and contrast between Stormfield's misinformed earthly expectations of a pinched Christian heaven and St. Peter's disclosure of a genuinely grand cosmic heaven. The perfect discrepancy between disclosure and expectation gives a perspective by incongruity, economizing the Captain's criticism of the puny Christian scheme and saving him from the trap of reform into which Hank Morgan's burlesque power disappeared. Moreover, there is a charge of good feeling running through the Captain's entire narrative, because St. Peter's grand disclosures amount to an expression of the Captain's own repressed hopes. The heaven to which he goes is a discovery almost too good to be true.

But there is a second reason which saved Stormfield from Morgan's fate. By posing the form as an extract, Mark Twain could not only break away from narrative responsibilities and expectations which required

From *Mark Twain and the Fate of Humor* (copyright © 1966 by Princeton University Press), pp. 291-293. Omission of footnotes. Reprinted by permission of Princeton University Press (title is editor's).

plot and sequence; he could hopefully convey the illusion that the extract was but the teasing surface of a forbidden reality which lay awaiting publication. The act of publication was thus an act which created possibilities offstage. Yet such a form, in order not to be the shallow evasion it played upon, had to meet one of two exacting requirements. Either it had to offer the kind of apparent fragmentation which, like the sketch, was actually the complete form; or it had to be a true extract and possess the unpublished reserve it advertised. To be great, it had to offer both. *Captain Stormfield's Visit to Heaven*—and similar extracts such as "Adam's Diary," and "Eve's Diary"—offered the first possibility but not the second. Beautifully effective workings of limited burlesque contrasts, they were able to break off abruptly the moment the contrast was exploited and the threat of repetition loomed.

WILLIAM M. GIBSON
THE IMAGINATIVE ACHIEVEMENT OF
"CAPTAIN STORMFIELD'S VISIT
TO HEAVEN"

"Captain Stormfield's Visit to Heaven" exists in three forms: a manuscript from the early 1870s with later additions and notebook entries, not all of them published; the middle chapters, which Mark Twain himself published after his wife's death as "Extracts from Captain Stormfield's Visit to Heaven," in *Harper's* in December 1907 and January 1908 and then in a Christmas gift book; and a second, fuller version published in 1952 [edited by Dixon Wecter] as Part I of *Report from Paradise*. It is unique among the Mark Twain stories in that he conceived the idea as early as 1868 and tinkered with the story almost to the time of his death; and it is a work of high imagination and vivid satire as well.

The Mark Twain *aficionado* will recognize Captain Stormfield almost at once. He is Capt. Hurricane Jones in "Rambling Notes of an Idle Excursion" (1877), Capt. Ned Blakely of *Roughing It* (1872), who demands and gets frontier justice for the murder of his Negro mate, and Captain

From *The Art of Mark Twain* (New York: Oxford University Press, 1976), pp. 83-89. Reprinted by permission (title is editor's).

Waxman, who tells about the fabulous rats that left a doomed ship (still earlier, in an *Alta California* letter). In real life he was Capt. Edgar (Ned) Wakeman, on whose steamship Mark Twain sailed to New York via the Isthmus of Panama in 1866, and with whom he again took passage when returning to California in 1868: a "portly, hearty, jolly, boisterous, good-natured sailor," a superior ship's captain, an expert interpreter of the Bible, and a yarn-spinner to rival Mark Twain himself [Wecter, p. xi]. It was on this second voyage that the Captain told his passenger of a visit he had made to heaven, his dream shading into reality as he had told it to many listeners in succession. Not long thereafter Mark Twain put the story germ on paper; and this was the beginning of his lifelong preoccupation with "Captain Stormfield" (p. xii). The dream visit fell in with another persistent interest of ex-Presbyterian Samuel Clemens: again and again in his writing he turned to heaven and hell, Adam and Eve, Satan and the Saviour, and the doctrines of election and predestination, although he had been in full revolt against all such since his adolescence.

In 1906 Mark Twain recalled writing down Captain Wakeman's experiences in heaven in "the first quarter of 1868, I think" (p. xii). This coincided with his reading—along with any number of his contemporaries—of Elizabeth Stuart Phelps Ward's novel *The Gates Ajar* (1868): she had turned the story, he says, into a burlesque of a book that had "imagined a mean little ten-cent heaven about the size of Rhode Island—a heaven large enough to accommodate about a tenth of one per cent of the Christian billions who had died in the past nineteen centuries. I raised the limit." Before he was through, that is, he was admitting pagans and measuring *his* heaven in light-years.

But *Gates Ajar* nonetheless meant much more to Mark Twain than a target for ridicule. Elizabeth Phelps, who had lost her lover in the Civil War, felt some of the same current of religious revolt that stirred in Clemens himself. The intellectual core of her novel, as distinguished from the strong emotional-sentimental strain, involves a fresh view of what heaven must be like. It protests any literal exegesis of *Revelation,* and of harps, choirs, the throne, robes, pearly gates, jewels, unending light, total exposure of the soul, idleness, solemnity—a place where "Sabbaths have no end." It is also aware of the speculation that the people who have lived and died would cover the earth twice over—or at least the state of Pennsylvania! For her part, Elizabeth Phelps, through the dialogue between the heroine and a sensitive aunt, proposes the possibility that heaven may be very much like the earth made spiritual. Perhaps the sun is the heaven of each system as Isaac Taylor had speculated. Though skeletons will surely not draw on their skins at the day of judgment, nor will human ashes be reconstituted, the human form divine will persist.

If there are no days, there will be succession of time. People will be busy there. If there are harpists, there will be pianists (a suggestion that surely shocked the orthodox among Mrs. Ward's readers). Who is to say that heaven will not have the animals in it?—Martin Luther thought that it might. Strikingly, heaven may be a place for those who failed on earth, and intellectual rank in heaven must bear some proportion to goodness. Above all, heaven will provide for talk, and for fun, and for books, and for good, and for the renewal of human love. How pleasant it will be, the heroine conjectures, to meet and perhaps even to shake the hand of David, or Paul, or Cowper, or President Lincoln, or Mrs. Browning.

The tone of Elizabeth Phelps's story is idealistic, consolatory, and often sentimental. But she read widely and was open to ideas, and plainly in *The Gates Ajar* she furnished Mark Twain more stimuli for events and ideas in "Captain Stormfield" than he was aware of or ever acknowledged.

Another real person furnished the prime satiric target of "Captain Stormfield." The Reverend Mr. T. DeWitt Talmage, minister of Brooklyn's Central Presbyterian Church, had observed in *The Independent* in 1870 that if all the churches were free and admitted working men, the uncommon people would be made sick by the bad smells of the common, so that he, Talmage, would have no part of this work of evangelization. This snobbery was just Mark Twain's meat. In reaction he wrote a very sharp piece for the *Galaxy,* calling it "About Smells" (May 1870). If laboring men from all the countries of the world—and this would include St. Matthew, Benjamin Franklin, the Twelve Apostles, and the Son of the Carpenter himself—are to be found in heaven, he asks, where will Mr. Talmage go? Elizabeth Phelps's bright young heroine had asked skeptically enough, "How can untold millions of us 'lie in Abraham's bosom'?" Talmage (so Captain Stormfield reports) avows in his sermons that the first thing he will do when he gets to heaven is to "fling his arms around Abraham, Isaac and Jacob, and kiss them and weep on them." But with sixty thousand people arriving every day, the patriarchs would "be tired out and as wet as muskrats all the time" (p. 586). No, says Stormfield, Mr. Talmage's endearments will be declined, with thanks.

In the longer printed version edited from manuscript by Dixon Wecter, "Captain Stormfield's Visit to Heaven" is really unfinished, like the other two versions; but most readers will feel content with the work as it stands, for it ends with a characteristic grand torchlight procession to celebrate the arrival in heaven of a "hard lot," a barkeeper from New Jersey. In the first quarter, a dramatic monologue addressed to the reader, Captain Eli Stormfield of San Francisco at his death whizzes off into outer space and through the sun, moving at 186,000 miles a second, as in a dream. . . . Stormfield . . . arrives in a heaven that accommodates Eskimos, Tartars,

Chinese, Mexicans, English, Arabs (very few white people), not to speak of a certain "sky-blue man with seven heads," from other universes (pp. 594, 572). The first narrative quarter concludes with a splendid race between Stormfield and a continent-sized comet. Stormfield in effect is winning the race—until he makes the mistake of thumbing his nose at the rival captain. The rival captain lightens ship by throwing overboard eighteen hundred thousand billion quintillion kazarks of brimstone—a kazark is the bulk of one hundred sixty-nine worlds—and soon disappears beyond Stormfield into the blackness of outer space (pp. 568-570).

The last three-quarters of the narrative are spieled off to "Peters" by Captain Stormfield, so that there is a listener for the storyteller; but Peters never responds, and Mark Twain manages his story of Stormfield in heaven mostly through dialogue between the captain and the head clerk, then a "nice old gent" named Sam, and finally bald-headed Sandy McWilliams. The ground for all this portion is simply a series of discoveries as to the true nature of the afterlife, all of them reversals of the conventional and expected.

The first blow to Stormfield's vanity is that the busy head clerk cannot identify San Francisco or the United States or the earth on the map of universes, which is as big as Rhode Island; and when the underclerk does find it, it is under the name of the Wart. The comet race, that is, had lasted long enough to divert Stormfield to a heavenly gate billions of leagues from the right one (pp. 571-573). This branch of heaven has no earthlings or harps or hymn-books in it; and heaven is both inconceivably large and immensely varied—as varied as its inhabitants. On reaching the corner of heaven for people from his own universe, Captain Stormfield is awarded "A harp and a hymn-book, pair of wings and a halo, size 13," by a Pi-Ute Injun gatekeeper whom he had known in Tulare County (p. 575). But it takes him only half a day of trying to fly and singing the only song he knows to discover from a new acquaintance, Sam, that heaven is *not* a haven of rest for "warbling ignoramuses" but just the "busiest place you ever heard of," where nothing harmless and reasonable is refused anybody. Heaven, Sam explains, has pain and suffering; but they do not last and they do not kill; without them, there could be no happiness. Above all, though the heavenly denizen must earn a thing to enjoy it, in heaven "you can choose your own occupation"; the shoemaker with the soul of a poet will in heaven be a poet (pp. 576-578).

Stormfield's education proceeds in heavenly discourse with the New Jersey angel, Sandy McWilliams. One picks his age after experiment, usually at the "place where his mind was last at its best," and one's intellect grows sharper in heaven, Sandy explains. The ideas are realized in the episode of a middle-aged, gray-haired mother's finding her child, who in twenty-seven years has grown into a philosopher, and learning to her sorrow that they have almost nothing in common any longer. They will come together, "but not this year, and not next," Sandy predicts. Pain and suffering, in short, are their lot, but not forever (pp. 579-583).

One of the unexpected and striking features of the hereafter, Captain Stormfield learns, is that it is a *kingdom*, where the prophets and patriarchs are deeply revered and are seen only on the rarest and greatest occasions. Just as there are paradoxes and discrepancies in Samuel Clemens's earlier views about caste and class ("Does the race of man love a lord?" Yes, and so in some fashion does Mark Twain), so they reappear in Stormfield's story. Sandy reveals how the heavenly inhabitants— apparently including himself—are awe-struck before the prophets and patriarchs. He makes it obvious, however, that earthly royalty take low status, and that heavenly justice prevails for the "mute inglorious Miltons" if not all the Pudd'nhead Wilsons of the earth; that the aristocracy of heaven is an *aristoi* of talent, not of rank or riches (pp. 587-591).

The drama and fun of this view take form in a series of characters, real and imagined. The Reverend Talmage of Brooklyn is here immortalized as a man who will never come near Abraham's bosom, or Jacob's or Isaac's either, though he had fully expected to weep there. The prophets, among them Homer and Shakespeare, take precedence over the patriarchs. Yet Billings, a tailor from Tennessee, whose poetry no one would print and who was ridden on a rail by his neighbors before his death, ranks above Homer and Shakespeare. More, the poets Saa, Bo, and Soof, from three different and remote systems, are known *throughout* heaven, as Homer, Shakespeare, and Billings are not. A certain Absalom Jones from the Boston back country, though he died obscure, was a greater military genius than Napoleon. Also, the sausage maker of Hoboken, Duffer by name, who fed the poor unobtrusively all his life, was greeted in heaven as Sir Richard Duffer, Baronet. Such, McWilliams tells Stormfield, is heavenly justice (pp. 590-593). In sum, Stormfield's heaven is a heaven on a liberal plan whose king, mentioned only once in reverence by the head clerk as the savior of uncounted worlds (p. 572), is like the Widow Douglas's Providence—generous and forgiving.

The work is touched by sentimentality and burlesque, but never more than briefly. It fails of any conventional ending. Yet is is surely one of Mark Twain's works of humane feeling and high imagination. One might in fact conclude that the tone of "Captain Stormfield's Visit to Heaven" is close to that of *Adventures of Huckleberry Finn.* Except for two "voyage" chapters written in 1901, it was complete in the early 1880s; so that, with the exception of the incomplete, totally different "Chronicle of Young Satan" (1897), never again was Mark Twain to write fiction so well.

9

THE MYSTERIOUS STRANGER

Mark Twain considered "The Mysterious Stranger," like "Captain Storm-field's Visit to Heaven," too shocking for his contemporaries to read but felt the world might be ready for it about one hundred years after his death. Only six years after he died, the story was published by Albert Bigelow Paine, his literary executor, in seven installments in *Harper's Mazagine,* beginning in the May issue of 1916, and somewhat inappropriately, as a children's Christmas book by Harper and Brothers, 1916.

Recently we have been shown, however, that the shock of the story was considerably blunted by its editors, Paine and Frederick A. Duneka of Harper's. In a fascinating piece of literary detective work, John S. Tuckey has provided a description of these editorial changes, as well as an accurate dating of the three manuscript versions of the story. These "Little Satan" manuscripts are now available in *Mark Twain's Mysterious Stranger Manuscripts,* edited by William M. Gibson. (University of California Press, 1969). Tuckey's account of his discoveries is included as the first selection in this section.

The remaining essays here merely update Tuckey's fine collection, *The Mysterious Stranger and the Critics.* Readers should consult his text for a full overview of the criticism on this story.

JOHN S. TUCKEY
"THE MYSTERIOUS STRANGER"
Mark Twain's Texts and the Paine-Duneka Edition

Left among Mark Twain's papers at the time of his death were three versions of a story of a mysterious stranger, a character of super-human powers. They are, as named and catalogued by Bernard DeVoto, the "Hannibal" mauscript of about fifteen thousand words; the "Eseldorf," of about fity-five thousand words; and the "Print Shop," of some sixty-five thousand words. All are in Mark Twain's own handwriting. There are also in existence typescripts of the "Eseldorf" and of the "Print Shop" manuscript, as prepared under Mark Twain's direction and revised by him. These manuscripts and typescripts are among the Mark Twain Papers at the General Library of the University of California at Berkeley. They are the same materials that were available to Albert Bigelow Paine, Mark Twain's official biographer and literary executor, and to Frederick A. Duneka, then general manager of Harper & Brothers, when they edited what was posthumously published in 1916 as *The Mysterious Stranger.* What these editors did in preparing the story for publication is itself a remarkable story.

Some idea of their massive editorial revisions can at once be suggested by saying that from the "Eseldorf" manuscript, used for all but the final brief chapter of *The Mysterious Stranger,* fully one-fourth of Mark Twain's wordage was deleted. One of Mark Twain's characters, Father Adolf, was partly edited out of the story, and another character, the astrologer, *whom Mark Twain did not have in his story at all,* was written in and made to perform most of the evil deeds that Mark Twain had attributed to Father Adolf, his intended villain.

The three versions are not so much different drafts of one story as three different stories. Each has for the most part different characters, situations, and actions. Even the mysterious strangers are differently characterized in each manuscript. Paine believed (and probably not mistakenly) that "Eseldorf" was the best of the versions. But the manuscript must have seemed to him quite unpublishable as it stood. The first chapter was largely devoted to a hostile characterization of the "dissolute and profane and malicious" priest—and Paine and Duneka were probably hoping to provide a new Mark Twain story that would be suitable for the

From *Mark Twain's "The Mysterious Stranger" and the Critics* by John S. Tuckey, editor. © 1948 by Wadsworth Publishing Company, Inc., Belmont, California 94002. Reprinted by permission of the publisher. Footnotes have been deleted.

Christmas trade! [See the author's *Mark Twain and Little Satan* (1963), pp. 17–21.] Furthermore, "Eseldorf" had no well-sustained plot; the tale became by turns a satire on religious hypocrisy, an allegory of human life as seen in miniature, a sermon on the moral sense and its degrading effect upon the species, a story of youthful romance and love rivalry, an exemplum of deterministic doctrines, a burlesqued philosophical dispute, and a long, long diatribe on the corruption of *fin de siècle* civilization—to mention only some of the more lengthy sections. Insofar as there was a basic plot, it concerned the finding of the gold coins by the good priest Father Peter; his arrest for a theft charged against him by the bad priest; his imprisonment and trial; his finding happiness at last in insanity. But there were some almost unrelated episodes. Modes and moods were as variable: the story was satiric, comic, sentimental, farcical, didactic. Clearly, it needed integration. Paine and Duneka were not overly concerned with such matters as preserving the purity—what there was of it—of their author's text. Mark Twain's adverse representations of Father Adolf were either toned down or taken out entirely; the astrologer was introduced as a more acceptable villain. Also almost entirely deleted was a long passage in which the young Satan vied with youths of the village of Eseldorf for the regard of Lilly and Marget, using his powers to outdo his rivals. Only one paragraph of this passage survives in *The Mysterious Stranger* [in Chapter 7, where it is related that Satan charmed Marget by reciting poetry and that Wilhelm Meidling became jealous]. Like some other sections that were cut out, this one was very much aside from the main plot; moreover, much of it was not in the sombre mood that Paine and Duneka tended to emphasize by deleting other kinds of material.

Although Paine and Duneka allowed a considerable part of Mark Twain's satire to remain in *The Mysterious Stranger,* they also deleted much of it. For example, they struck from the typescript of "Eseldorf" that was used as the printer's copy for the published story more than forty pages of satiric commentary on civilization in the late nineteenth century. Moreover, they blunted or obscured much of the satire that was retained by omitting the specific objects of Mark Twain's attack. Explicit references to the Boer War, the actions of the Allied Powers in China, and the Spanish-American War were all carefully omitted. Printing the author's fulminations against wartime hypocrisies and atrocities without letting him say just what had provoked them tended to make Mark Twain appear bitter without sufficient grounds for bitterness, more despairing than there was any evident reason for being; in a word, pessimistic.

The "Eseldorf" manuscript also lacked an ending. But Paine had found a manuscript fragment that he believed to be Mark Twain's intended conclusion for *The Mysterious Stranger*. In his introduction to the story in the Definitive Edition, Paine related that one day at Stormfield (Mark Twain's home at Redding from June 1908 until his death) the author had said to him, "I always had a good deal of fancy for that story of mine, 'The Mysterious Stranger.' I could finish it, I suppose, any time, and I should like it some day to be published." Paine also recalled, "A considerable time after his death—after the publication of my biography of him . . . I found among a confusion of papers that tremendous final chapter, which must have been written about the time of our conversation. It may even have been written prior to that time, laid aside and forgotten, for his memory was very treacherous during those later days." He added, "Happily, it was the ending of the story in its first form."

Actually, as I have attempted to demonstrate in another context, there is strong evidence that Mark Twain wrote "that tremendous final chapter" in 1904, while he was living at Florence during Olivia's last illness. There is also positive evidence that he wrote it as a conclusion for the "Print Shop" version. The characters named in it, August and "44," are respectively the narrator and the mysterious stranger of "Print Shop." These names were struck out and the names "Theodor" and "Satan" were inserted—in what appears to be Paine's handwriting. [See *Mark Twain and Little Satan*, p. 61.] Paine allowed himself to speak somewhat loosely in saying that the ending was that "of the story in its first form," since he believed (and rightly) that "Eseldorf" was the earliest version, and since he knew that the characters in Mark Twain's conclusion were not those of "Eseldorf." But if he had attempted to say anything at all about textual alterations, he might have had to say a great deal. And it must be remembered that Mark Twain had not yet become very much the concern of the scholarly; Paine would hardly have thought it needful to give an account that would interest textual critics.

Some further tinkering was needed to make the "Print Shop" ending fit the "Eseldorf" manuscript. Two transitional paragraphs were added— apparently while *The Mysterious Stranger* was in proof. The last paragraph of Chapter 10 and the first paragraph of Chapter 11 cannot be found in either the "Eseldorf" holograph or in the typescript that went to the printer. In all probability it was Paine who composed the transitional paragraphs, and one can admire his deftness if not his presumption. What he wrote is sufficiently in keeping with Mark Twain's own habits of thought and expression. Indeed, one writer [Edward Stone in *Voices of Despair*, 1966] has partly based a critical point regarding Mark Twain's pessimism on that editorially supplied last paragraph of Chapter 10. He ventures to find, in the comparison of Satan's attitude toward human beings to a naturalist's interest in a collection of ants, an indication that

Mark Twain was drawing upon his reading of John Lubbock's *Ants, Bees, and Wasps* and Charles Darwin's *The Descent of Man.* His point may still hold well enough, for the paragraph is quite passably, though not actually, Twainian. It should nevertheless be noted that the Paine-Duneka edition does have its pitfalls for literary critics.

Such traps are always likely to exist when a text deviates from the author's intended forms and usages. And it is perhaps only a mild exaggeration to say that the Paine-Duneka edition is about as far from Mark Twain's own latest intended form of *The Mysterious Stranger* as it would, on any ordinary working day, be possible to get. Paine, it has been seen, used what he believed (correctly) to be the *earliest* version—and gave the impression that even the concluding "Print Shop" chapter was written for that version. He explained that the other, *later* forms of the story were "lacking in interest, being mainly wanderings in those fantastic fields into which Mark Twain was prone to be tempted." Although he underrated the interest of these other versions, Paine was probably right about the superior literary quality of the manuscripts he and Duneka used. In good time the world will be able to judge, for the three versions as Mark Twain wrote them will presently be available in a volume of the Mark Twain Papers series as prepared for publication by Professor William M. Gibson. That volume will be of great value for biographical and critical study, for it will reveal much about Mark Twain's processes of literary creation; it will also invite, indeed demand, comparison with the Paine-Duneka edition. But in any case *The Mysterious Stranger* not only does not represent Mark Twain's own intended form of the manuscripts on which it was based; it also does not represent Mark Twain's latest intended version of his story of a mysterious stranger. Moreover, the only version that Mark Twain himself seems ever to have *called* "The Mysterious Stranger" is the "Print Shop" manuscript. His title for the "Eseldorf" version had been "The Chronicle of Young Satan"; and he had designated the "Hannibal" version as the "Story of little Satan Jr. who came to Hannibal." When he took the initial chapter from the "Eseldorf" manuscript (after abandoning work on that version) and used it in beginning "Print Shop," he crossed out his original title and wrote "The Mysterious Stranger" as the name of his latest version.

It was the "Print Shop" version that Mark Twain was writing when he referred to his work on "The Mysterious Stranger" in letters and memoranda of the summer and fall of 1905. And it was that version that he would have had in mind in his dictation of August 30, 1906, when, after speaking of some of his half-finished books, he said, "There is yet another—*The Mysterious Stranger.* It is more than half finished. I would dearly like to finish it, and it causes me a real pang to reflect that it is not to be." He was, he said, "tired of the pen."

That Paine and Duneka did not publish Mark Twain's own intended form of *The Mysterious Stranger* was not made evident by Bernard DeVoto's interpretations as put forward in his generally perceptive psychological study "The Symbols of Despair" [in *Mark Twain at Work*, 1942]. Although he acknowledged that he had not been able to date many of Mark Twain's later manuscripts and that he could not be sure of their chronology, DeVoto did perforce assume a chronology. But he believed that the "Eseldorf" version was the *latest* form of *The Mysterious Stranger* and that it had been written about 1905, marking the restoration of Mark Twain's literary talent after seven or eight barren years. There is evidence, however, that "Eseldorf" was indeed the earliest version, as Paine had thought, and that Mark Twain began it late in 1897 and at that time carried the tale well into the fifth chapter. He then wrote the brief "Hannibal" version in November 1898, between spurts of work on "Eseldorf." He worked again upon the "Eseldorf" manuscript in the fall of 1899 and again in the summer of 1900, and then abandoned it (references to contemporary events make firm datings possible). During several working periods between the fall of 1902 and the summer of 1905, he wrote the "Print Shop" version. He composed the greater part in 1904, and wrote the seven-hundred-word "Print Shop" ending, proclaiming life to be *"only a vision, a dream,"* in the spring or summer of that year. Thus *The Mysterious Stranger* as published was, except for the last few hundred words, written not about 1905 but between 1897 and 1900, or during what DeVoto believed had been the lowest ebb of Mark Twain's literary ability. It was exactly during this supposed time of impotence and failure that Mark Twain composed all but one brief fragment of what DeVoto called in his introduction to *The Portable Mark Twain*, "an almost perfect book—perfect in expression of his final drive, in imaginative projection of himself, in tone and tune, in final judgment"—*The Mysterious Stranger.*

DeVoto was nearly silent regarding the gross revisions of Paine and Duneka. He wrote as if *The Mysterious Stranger* had been published just as Mark Twain had written it—except for the addition of the brief final chapter, which he regarded as Paine's greatest service to Mark Twain. Presumably he had examined "Eseldorf" closely enough to realize how very much it differed from the Paine-Duneka edition; yet it seems curious that he did not credit those collaborators, or coauthors, for a more considerable part of the supposed perfection of the story as published. His reticences, following those of Paine, have allowed an extraordinary textual problem to remain, for half a century, almost unrecognized.

The Paine-Duneka edition is really so different from the mauscripts upon which it was based that it is in some measure a fourth version, a collaborative creation. Despite its imperfections, it is also the only existing form of the story that has the coherence and completeness of a realized literary work ("Print Shop" has an ending—the only ending—but is lacking in integration; "Hannibal" is hardly more than a beginning). Corrupt as it is, the Paine-Duneka edition has held a place in our literature for more than half a century. Generally regarded as the most important work of Mark Twain's later years, it has received and is receiving much critical attention. Here, then, is the problem: to what extent must the merit and validity of such a literary creation depend upon its textual authority? *The Odyssey* is still *The Odyssey* no matter how many Homers it took to create it. To be sure, *The Mysterious Stranger* is no *Odyssey,* and Paine and Duneka are less than Homeric. But does the Paine-Duneka edition, under the existing circumstances, deserve to perish, to endure, or to prevail?

JOHN R. MAY

THE GOSPEL ACCORDING TO PHILIP TRAUM
Structural Unity in "The Mysterious Stranger"

The major problem with the criticism of "The Mysterious Stranger" to date is that it has been too narrowly concerned with a thematic justification of the last chapter in relation to the rest of the work. The story was unfinished at the time of Twain's death; and it was not until his literary executor, Albert Bigelow Paine, "discovered" the final chapter that the story was eventually published in 1916. Without a final chapter the story undoubtedly lacks a sense of direction, yet critics have had trouble justifying the relationship between the unambiguous solipsism of the last chapter and the earlier development of the story. Is there any preparation in the story for the utter negation of external reality that Philip Traum's revelation in the last chapter represents?

In *Mark Twain and Little Satan,* published in 1963, John S. Tuckey establishes conclusively the order of Twain's composition of the three distinct versions of the Satan story, that Bernard DeVoto had previously

From *Studies in Short Fiction,* 8 (1971), 411–422. Reprinted by permission of the author and by the editor of *Studies.*

named—the Eseldorf Version, the edited text that was actually published; the Hannibal Version, describing the influence of a young Statan named "44" on Tom Sawyer and Huck Finn; and the Print Shop Version, concerned again with "44," but as the dream self of August Feldner. One of Tuckey's conclusions is that Paine's last chapter is actually the conclusion to the Print Shop Version; but since the Eseldorf text was clearly the most developed manuscript, he made the necessary editorial changes so that the Print Shop conclusion would fit the Eseldorf story. His thesis seems to have had little impact on the present state of criticism of the novel; there is obvious need, therefore, for serious critical study of the manuscripts. The publication of *Mark Twain's Mysterious Stranger Manuscripts* (University of California, 1969), edited by William M. Gibson, will no doubt aid this process. The volume contains the three fragmentary versions, with notes concerning the appearance of the manuscripts and all emendations, cancellations, marginalia—and in whose handwriting. As interesting and informative as these textual investigations will be, though, perhaps criticism will in the final analysis simply have to accept Paine's 1916 version as a kind of literary "fortunate fall"—a masterful piece of editing and, because of its extraordinary power, a work of art in its own right.

The most satisfactory attempts to discover unity in the present manuscript have concentrated on the relationship between the first ten chapters and the conclusion; and since the conclusion is so openly didactic and philosophical, these studies have focused on the thematic development in the earlier chapters. Edwin Fussell finds a coherent development in the story to its solipsistic conclusion; it represents, he says, an objectification of the mental process whereby Theodor discards his mistaken belief in the reality of the world for an acceptance of the reality of dreams alone. (His essay published ten years before Tuckey's rejection of the last chapter, justifies the acceptance of the Paine conclusion on the grounds that Twain did after all write the chapter; whether he liked it or not, says Fussell, is beside the point.) Pascal Covici thinks that "the most salient feature of *The Mysterious Stranger* is that Theodor's point of view changes and changes radically." William C. Spengemann, seeing this last major work of Twain's in relation to *Tom Sawyer* and *Huckleberry Finn*, believes that the final chapter can be taken as the "logical conclusion" of the events which precede it if it is interpreted in terms of "escape from life in cosmic innocence."

The excellence of these studies is nonetheless marred by the fact that the excessive concern for justifying the final chapter has forced them to be selective. They concentrate on the thematic development of the novella and thereby ignore much of the richness and coherence of the narrative structure. It is hard to see, for example, how their conclusions concerning the thematic unity of the story answer the objections raised by Edmund Reiss. "Although beginning auspiciously," he writes, "the novelette tends to become disjointed. The questions of the worth of man, of the ambiguity of good and evil, of the Moral Sense, begin to fade into the background as Twain emphasizes the adventurous part of the story. . . . Incidents that are interesting but distracting begin to appear. In not contributing much to the whole work, many of Theodor's adventures . . . are . . . satirical, curious, but yet, as they stand, not really necessary. It is with the final chapter that 'The Mysterious Stranger' regains the intensity of its opening episodes."

Any satisfactory treatment of the unity of the story will, therefore, have to go beyond the thematic development to show, if possible, how the whole narrative contributes to the development of the discerned underlying theme. It is with this purpose in mind that I offer the following observations concerning the structural unity of "The Mysterious Stranger."

Coleman O. Parsons is credited with making the connection between the portrayal of Satan and the Jesus of the New Testament Apocrypha; there are clear references in Mark Twain's notebook to the impression that the discovery of the Apocryphal Gospels made upon him. His indebtedness to the New Testament, however, whether conscious or unconscious, goes beyond the similarity of characterization. For if there is any principle of structural unity in "The Mysterious Stranger," it is a variation of the Gospel form, which frequently—as in Matthew—juxtaposes the actions and discourses of Jesus within the pattern of his ministry of salvation. In the light of this, "The Mysterious Stranger" becomes a kind of anti-Gospel because the news that it brings is not a celebration of reality but of negation.

The structural unity of "The Mysterious Stranger" develops out of Philip Traum's mission of salvation to Theodor Fischer. The narrative context of this educational process is circumscribed by Traum's three attempts to help Fr. Peter and his household—first, by giving Fr. Peter money to pay his debts; then, by helping Ursula and Marget while Fr. Peter is in jail; and finally, by possessing Wilhelm Meidling during his defense of Fr. Peter at the trial. A moral lesson, presented in the form of a discourse, is drawn from the circumstances surrounding each of these actions—which is rendered universal for Theodor's instruction by Traum's manipulation of time and space. One can demonstrate that all of the narrative lies within this threefold framework, either as descriptive preparation for or dramatic consequence of the action taken, or as illustrative of Satan's discourses. For the purpose of describing the three segments of the story, it seems advisable to consider the whole novel first, on the level of action and discourse, and only then to treat the significance of the threefold excursion into time and space.

The narrative is set in a dreamy Austrian village in 1590. Austria itself was asleep, we are told; and Eseldorf "was in the middle of that sleep, being in the middle of Austria. . . . It was still the Middle Ages in Austria, and promised to remain so forever" (p. 602). The medieval atmosphere of the village is accentuated as the narrator describes successively the castle, the absent prince, the importance of Christian training, the two priests, the astrologer, and the "inquisition."

The finely-sketched introduction quickly reveals the situation out of which the three narrative strands will develop. Fr. Peter has been charged "with talking around in conversation that God was all goodness and would find a way to save all of his poor human children" (p. 603). The astrologer, Fr. Peter's open enemy—and "a very powerful one" (*ibid.*)— because he impressed the bishop with his piety, was suspected of reporting Fr. Peter's statement to the bishop. Despite pleas for mercy from the priest's niece, Marget, the bishop "suspended Fr. Peter indefinitely" (p. 604). For two years Fr. Peter has been without his flock, and he and his niece are in serious financial difficulty.

The way is prepared for the appearance of a savior. The morning after a nocturnal encounter with a ghost at the castle, Theodor Fischer and his inseparable companions, Seppi Wohlmeyer and Nikolaus Bauman, are talking over the experiences of the previous evening, in the shade of a nearby woody hilltop, when a youth comes strolling toward them through the trees. The handsome stranger tries to put the boys at ease by miraculously providing the fire that they need to be able to smoke. He says that his name is Satan, even though he is really only Satan's nephew. When he is trying to conceal his identity, he uses the name Philip Traum.

Satan quickly commands the attention and interest of the boys by creating some tiny people whom he later wantonly destroys because they begin to argue and fight. Satan's powers both charm and frighten the boys, They are charmed by his creative ingenuity, yet appalled by his merciless destruction of the people he has created. From a narrative viewpoint, this passage serves the purpose of establishing his credentials as one who can achieve the miraculous; it also provides the opportunity for Satan to introduce the thesis of his first discourse: that man is the victim of the moral sense—"a sense whose function is to distinguish between right and wrong, with liberty to choose which of them he will do." "He is always choosing," Satan insists, "and in nine cases out of ten he prefers the wrong" (p. 628). This thesis will be developed throughout the first phase of the narrative, which is concerned with the events resulting from Satan's gift to Fr. Peter.

Thus, when Fr. Peter recovers his lost wallet in the presence of the boys and finds it filled with money, the boys know immediately the source of the money—even though they cannot tell because Satan will not allow them to reveal his identity. They nevertheless persuade Fr. Peter to keep the money and use it to pay his debts, until the rightful owner can be found.

The people attribute his good fortune "to the plain hand of Providence" (p. 618). The ironic interplay of reality and belief is humorously suggested when one or two of the citizens say privately that "it looked more like the hand of Satan," and Theodor observes that "really that seemed a surprisingly good guess for ignorant people like that" (*ibid*). Celebrating Fr. Peter's good fortune, the boys approach him to ask what the moral sense is. Fr. Peter's answer that "it is the one thing that lifts man above the beasts that perish and makes him heir to immortality" leaves the boys "filled but not fatted" (p. 619).

Fr. Peter's prosperity is short-lived, though. Accused by the astrologer of stealing his money, Fr. Peter is put in jail; and his niece and the household are again reduced to penury. Concerned about Fr. Peter, Theodor thinks that he would like to see the jail; and he and Satan are there the next moment because Satan reads his thought. A young man accused of heresy is being tortured on a rack, and Theodor calls it "a brutal thing." Satan's response is a further elaboration of the perversity of the moral sense. "No, it was a human thing," he reminds Theodor; "you should not insult brutes by such a misuse of that word. . . . No brute ever does a cruel thing—that is the monopoly of those with the moral sense" (p. 628). As a further illustration of the point, Satan takes Theodor to a French factory "where men and women and little children were toiling in heat and dirt and a fog of dust" (p. 629). Satan explains: "It is the Moral Sense which teaches the factory proprietors the difference between right and wrong—you perceive the result" (p. 629). The next moment they are back on the streets of Eseldorf and hearing from Seppi about the mysterious disappearance of Hans Oppert, who has not been seen since he "brutally" struck his faithful dog and knocked out one of his eyes. Satan reminds them "that brutes do not act like that, but only men" (p. 630). His lesson concerning the moral sense is ironically heightened by the fact that the dog, despite his beatings, has been trying in vain to direct the villagers to his dying master; but no one pays any attention to the dog, and Hans dies without absolution.

At this point in the narrative, though, the second strand has already been introduced because as soon as Fr. Peter is imprisoned, Satan helps his household again by giving Ursula, Fr. Peter's servant, the Lucky Cat— "whose owner finds four silver groschen in his pocket every morning"

(p. 625). This overlapping of narrative strands is no indication of lack of artistic control, but rather a technique of heightened artistic effect parallel to the overlapping statements of the melody in a fugue.

Human nature being what it is, Ursula hires young Gottfried Narr to help around the house—now that there is an abundance of money. The boys wonder, though, about the wisdom of this decision because Gott-fried's grandmother had been burned as a witch, and "the witch-terror had risen higher during the past year than it had ever reached in the memory of the oldest villagers" (p. 632). Theodor tells Satan about Gottfried's grandmother and about eleven schoolgirls all of whom the commission had forced to confess to practicing witchcraft. Satan answers by calling a bullock out of a pasture and emphasizing the fact that animals, like angels, do not have the moral sense and therefore "wouldn't drive children mad with hunger and fright and loneliness," nor would they "break the hearts of innocent, poor old women" (p. 634).

Again Providence was "getting all the gratitude" (p. 636) for the tem-porary well-being of Fr. Peter's household. But Fr. Adolf and the astrologer begin to suspect witchcraft, especially after Gottfried's remark in the presence of the latter that Marget and Ursula were "living on the fat of the land" (p. 635). When other means of detecting witchcraft have failed, they decide that they will use the party Marget has announced as an opportunity to discover with certainty the source of the household's abundance. When they see the house filled with delicacies, knowing that no supplies were brought in all week, they are convinced that it is "witch-craft . . . of a new kind—a kind never dreamed of before" (p. 638). Satan intervenes, though, to cast suspicion back on the astrologer and Fr. Adolf. The situation deteriorates when the possessed astrologer performs stunts in the market square beyond his age and powers. So rampant now is the fear of witchcraft that the townspeople are convinced that God has for-saken them.

These events lead directly into Satan's second discourse. Theodor feels that he has to try to reform Satan and begs him "to be more considerate and stop making people unhappy" (p. 643). They are in China at the time, and Satan explains to Theodor that there is nothing that can be done about the happiness quotient in a human's life. "Every man is a suffering-machine and a happiness-machine combined" (pp. 643-644); and either happiness and suffering are equally divided, or suffering predominates. The principal point of this discourse and of the events that follow it by way of illustration through Chapter Eight seems to be that there is so much necessary misery in human life that death comes as a genuine favor to victimized humanity. The determinism that is preached here does not, as some critics have suggested, imply a denial of the freedom that is necessary to make the perversity of man's moral sense deliberate; it is rather a determinism to misery. If there is any lack of freedom, it is not the freedom of moral choice, but rather the freedom to choose happiness over misery. As a corollary to his instruction concerning the mercy of death in the light of human misery, Satan anticipates his ultimate denial of the reality of an afterlife by denying the existence of purgatory and implying that there is no heaven.

The whole discussion of the inexorable sequence of man's acts—like the toppling of bricks laid in a row—is placed within the context of man's inability to know good fortune from bad because he cannot see into the future, where there is nothing but misery. Man's "first childish act" (p. 647), which situates him in particular circumstances, in a certain environment, can hardly be important from a moral point of view; it is simply the origin of his misery because it is the beginning of a life that only death can happily terminate. Satan, who can see all the possible careers open to an individual, knows that the only favor that can be done for a human being is either to terminate his life or to make him insane. The subsequent events in this second strand illustrate the mercy of death; in the third strand of the narrative, Satan will resort to insanity as salvation for Fr. Peter.

The conclusion of the second part of the story deals in some detail with the changes that Satan effects in the lives of Nikolaus, Frau Brandt, and Fischer the weaver. Of the three, only Fischer's life is lengthened; the defect in the change is the terrifying implication for Theodor that as a result of his new career Fischer will go to hell. Finally, the vision of human history from its beginning into the future, with no one but a "parcel of usurping monarchs and nobilities" (p. 663) profiting from life, fortifies the lesson of human misery.

The third strand of the narrative focuses on the trial: Satan's victory for Fr. Peter through the defense by Wilhelm Meidling and the doctrine of laughter that Satan preaches as the only enduring antidote to the absurdities of life. The witch-commission, at first, is afraid to proceed against Fr. Peter and the astrologer—no doubt because of the esteem the village holds for both of them. Instead they hang a poor, friendless women, while a mob throws stones at her. Satan bursts out laughing, and his laughter is clearly significant. The crowd demands to know why he laughed and especially why he threw no stone. After answering his three accusers with the announcement of their imminent deaths, Satan admits to Theodor that he was actually laughing at him for throwing stones while his "heart revolted at the act" (p. 666). Distrust of neighbors and fear of reprisals had led the mob to be ruled by the malicious few.

When Fr. Peter eventually comes to trial, Satan possesses Wilhelm and, by demonstrating from the date on the coins that they could not belong to the astrologer, wins Fr. Peter's freedom. But the happiness that he had promised Theodor he would gain for Fr. Peter is the happiness of insanity, for he lies to Fr. Peter and tells him that he has been found guilty and been disgraced—and the shock dislodges the old man's reason. When Theodor reproaches Satan for his lie, Satan explains his action: "Are you so unobservant as not to have found out that sanity and happiness are an impossible combination? No sane man can be happy, for to him life is real, and he sees what a fearful thing it is. Only the mad can be happy, and not many of those" (pp. 673-674).

Satan's third discourse follows immediately; it is an explanation of his laughter during the stoning episode as well as a corollary to his observations on insanity and happiness. The human race, he insists, lacks a genuine sense of humor. They see "the comic side of a thousand low-grade and trivial . . . incongruities"—another example of the "continuous and uninterrupted self-deception" that enslaves the race, but they miss thereby "the ten-thousand high-grade comicalities which exist in the world" (p. 674). The only antidote to these radical inconsistencies is to "laugh at them—and by laughing at them destroy them" (*ibid*). He concludes: "Against the assault of laughter nothing can stand" (*ibid.*). We understand now the curious rationality behind his salvation of Fr. Peter. Both laughter and insanity negate reality; but since the race lacks the courage to laugh, insanity was the only sure redemption for Fr. Peter.

The excursion to India is the last narrative episode of the story; and although it seems somehow unequal to its climactic position in the narrative, it does nevertheless serve as a summary illustration of Satan's Gospel. The foreigner, a Portuguese colonist, refuses to allow the natives to enjoy the fruit of Satan's tree even for an hour because the tree is on his property. The natives respond with humble obeisance to their master. Only the moral sense can explain the foreigner's perversity, and the misery of the groveling natives is another example of the foolish acceptance of the master-slave relationship which "is the foundation upon which all civilizations have been built" (p. 663). The foreigner will conceal his acceptance of the sentence Satan has imposed upon him—for fear of the natives. Only by preventing their revenge can he secure his ascendancy over them. The "high-grade" incongruity of the foreigner's situation is that he will "fetch a priest to cast out the tree's devil" (p. 677). Of course, the priest's incantations will be ineffectual; such belief itself is the ultimate incongruity of the race because it is patently groundless.

Before discussing the final chapter in relationship to the narrative as it has unfolded thus far, we must consider the cosmic dimension added to the narrative structure by the threefold excursion into time and space.

"It was wonderful," Theodor exclaims at the beginning of Chapter Nine, "the mastery Satan had over time and distance" (p. 664). An overview of Twain's method of universalizing the lessons learned through the process of Fr. Peter's salvation is crucial to a proper understanding of the function of the controversial last chapter.

Each of Satan's three discourses is applied to all of humanity—in space and in time. In the first strand, the journey to the French factory becomes a spatial confirmation of the universal perversity of man's moral sense. The temporal expansion of the discourse is achieved by Satan's symbolic repetition of the creation of the world. The sequence of miracles by which he establishes his angelic powers (which are really more divine than angelic, according to any traditional theological model)—fire, ice, fruit, animals, and finally men—corresponds roughly to the order of creation found in the first chapter of Genesis—light, firmament, plants, animals, and man. There would seem to be no other reason for this succession of miracles, in precisely this order, than to take us back in time to the very origin of man's problem—his creation as a being endowed with the moral sense.

The setting of the second discourse is China, as far removed from Eseldorf as is spatially conceivable on this planet. We may conjecture that the reason "why Satan chose China for this excursion instead of another place" (p. 643) is that he has thereby encircled the globe with his doctrine of necessary human misery, determined by the very fact of our existence in this world. The temporal excursion during this portion encompasses the whole of human history from Cain through the present and then "two or three centuries" into the future of the race, exhibiting only "a mighty procession" (p. 663) of slaughter and oppression.

The third discourse deals with the capacity of laughter to annul the appalling incongruities of reality. The last spatial excursion is to India and Ceylon; and the episode that occurs is, as we have seen, weakly illustrative of Philip Traum's total vision of the human race. The location, though, suggests the aura of mysticism characteristic of that area of the world—a perfect prelude to the final encounter between Theodor and Satan. The last chapter and its announcement of the dream quality of reality becomes the temporal conclusion to the story. To be fully understood within the structure of the work, it must be seen—in juxtaposition to creation at the beginning of the narrative—as the apocalypse of the end of time. We can see now more clearly, too, the progression from insanity through laughter to dream—since the proclamation that all reality is nothing but a dream is, of course, the theoretical ultimate in this series of views destructive of reality.

Understood as apocalypse, the final chapter both completes the temporal progression of the story and helps us to comprehend the nature of the change that has come over Theodor, because there can be no doubt that there is a qualitative difference between their encounter in the last chapter and their relationship until then. If we trace the development of Theodor's attitude toward Satan through the three stages of the narrative, we find that he moves from a period of profound shock at Satan's indifference to humanity, to a desire to reform Satan's ways, and finally to an attitude of diminished grief and private disapproval of Satan's actions. When Satan's lie has resulted in Fr. Peter's insanity, Theodor reflects: "Privately I did not think much of his processes" (p. 674). And after Satan's punishment of the Portuguese land-owner, he admits that it grieved him, "though not sharply, to see [Satan] take such a malicious satisfaction in his plans" (p. 677) for the foreigner. There is no simple linear development in Theodor's acceptance of Satan's shocking vision of humanity.

The level of response that we have traced thus far is primarily concerned with Satan's attitude and the consequent harshness of his actions. Running throughout the story, though, is the far more important motif of the boys' personal attachment to Philip. The enchantment of the person —the lure of his music, the excitement of his presence, and the ecstasy of his wine from heaven—is pronounced from the beginning and only grows in intensity as the story unfolds. "He made us drunk with the joy of being with him, and of looking into the heaven of his eyes, and of feeling the ecstasy that thrilled our veins from the touch of his hand" (p. 611). It is undoubtedly this attachment to the power of Philip's personality that becomes the ground for Theodor's leap of faith in accepting his final revelation.

But Satan himself is a dream and nothing more. How are we to understand this subtler aspect of the final revelation? "I am but a dream— your dream, creature of your imagination. . . . I, your poor servant, have revealed you to yourself and set you free. Dream other dreams, and better!" (p. 678). The dream that has uttered a final and definitive "No!" to reality is a dream that is conditioned by the age of belief—and which denies the reality of God, heaven, hell, the human race, and the universe. What is rejected here by Theodor's imagination is quite simply, but emphatically the Christian explanation of existence. But it is also more than this. It is a rejection of any reality outside of the self. Theodor is nothing more than "a vagrant thought, . . . wandering forlorn among the empty eternities!" (p. 679). The only better dream, then, that he can presumably dream is laughter.

We are left, finally, with the evident incongruity of an adolescent solipsist. However, even though the first person point of view is used, the story is narrated in the past tense—which indicates the passage of time between the actual occurrence of the events and the time of narration. Despite the fact that an effort is made to maintain the youthful point of view, there are certain passages where the age of the narrator shows through. In the opening paragraph, the narrator indicates that the Austria of the story is a remembrance, but that he remembers it well even though he was "only a boy" (p. 602). In recalling his last days with Nick, he notes: "It was an awful eleven days; and yet, with a lifetime stretching back between today and then, they are still a grateful memory to me, and beautiful" (p. 653). In Chapter Ten, while commenting on the fact that Satan seemed to know of no other way to do a person a favor except "by killing him or making a lunatic out of him," he adds: "Privately, I did not think much of his processes—*at that time*" (p. 674, my emphasis). And during Satan's final revelation, there is the patently adult exclamation: "By God! I had had that very thought a thousand times in my musings" (p. 678). Rather than consider these as lapses from the established viewpoint, as some critics have done, it seems more reasonable to explain them as intended emphasis of the passage of time. It certainly makes it easier for us to understand and accept the final vision of reality if we realize that it is an old man who is reflecting the bitterness of age, or at least a process of many years.

If Mark Twain has treated us to a harshly solipsistic view of reality, he has not done so without a sense of humor. Moreover, he has sweetened his anti-Gospel with the nostalgia of youth and given the vision artistic distance by setting the story in the remote past of our belief. And then he has, of course, left us with laughter.

RAYMOND VARISCO
DIVINE FOOLISHNESS
A Critical Evaluation of Mark Twain's "The Mysterious Stranger"

In *Sam Clemens of Hannibal,* Dixon Wector hypothesizes that as Twain's "dream" of boyhood innocence faded his stories dealing with boys tended to go unfinished. Certainly this seems to be a valid observation in view of

From *Revista/Review Interamericana,* 5 (Winter 1975-76), 741-749. Reprinted with the permission of the author and Inter American University of Puerto Rico.

the incomplete later works centering around Tom Sawyer and Huckleberry Finn. As recently as December of 1968, *Life* magazine published such an incomplete manuscript entitled "Huck Finn and Tom Sawyer Among the Indians." However, even as early as *Adventures of Huckleberry Finn* Twain's concept of innocence seems to have altered somewhat from the relatively simplistic notions of boyhood that he espouses in *Adventures of Tom Sawyer*. Tom is able to escape into fantasy whenever he wishes; and, although Tom has a great admiration for the foot-loose Huck, Tom's attitudes are the conventional attitudes of his community. He is, perhaps more than any other of Twain's innocent characters, a typical representative of his time and place. Tom is, after all, a composite drawn from many boys Twain claims to have known in his own childhood. To question anything like the morality of slavery never enters the mind of such a typical character. He accepts the opinions of his elders. Huck, on the other hand, is no ordinary boy. It is precisely Huck's rejection of the opinions of his elders and indeed his almost categorical rejection of adult society, as a whole, which form the core of *Huckleberry Finn*. Huck cannot escape into fantasy as easily as Tom. Huck is too much of a realist to do so; and his innocence is far more complex than Tom's. Twain's faded "dream" of boyhood is not, then, an exclusive product of his advancing years. Twain's life-long concern with the illusions and realities of childhood—the conflict of innocence and experience—is evident in *Huck Finn* as well as in later, unfinished works; and in the early as well as late works, Twain seems to speak with a multiplicity of narrative voices. These voices, as Hudson Long observes, mark Twain as a "romanticist and idealist on one hand, . . satirist and pessimist on the other."

Twain exhibits both idealistic and pessimistic attitudes throughout his career as an artist. If the pessimism seems finally to dominate his work it is only because his view of the world, which was constantly changing, seems ultimately to have presented before him a damned, rather than a saved, human race; and nowhere perhaps are the many facets of Twain's artistic perspective more visible than in "The Mysterious Stranger"—a tale in which Twain seems to embody all of his ultimate attitudes on man. In "The Stranger" Twain displays man as he appears before the innocent eyes of Theodor Fischer, and he displays man, that "puny creature," as he appears before the harsh and impersonal eyes of Satan.

Perhaps because of this dual vision of man, "The Stranger," of all the shorter works, early or late, is in many ways the most puzzling of the tales; and critical opinion varies widely as to the story's artistic merit. E. S. Fussell, for example, refers to the work as a "sulphurous little fairy tale," and he calls it Twain's "most audacious fictional venture." Coleman Parsons praises the tale and compares it, for somewhat obscure reasons, to Gray's "Ode on a Distant Prospect of Eton College." More in keeping with Fussell's opinion, J. R. Vitelli accuses the author of "The Stranger" and "The Man That Corrupted Hadleyburg" of forgetting "the lesson in humility he had learned on the Mississippi." Vitelli sounds almost as if he believes that the Mark Twain who wrote "The Stranger" and "Hadleyburg" was not the same Mark Twain who wrote *Life on the Mississippi* and *Tom Sawyer*. Fussell seems to share such a view, for he finally refers to "The Stranger" as a work which is "sorrowfully inexpressive of [Twain's] total orientation to life."

The tale of Eseldorf has been called fatalistic, misanthropic, solipsistic, and pure bunkum; and yet the critics who see the work as an expression of what Louis D. Rubin calls Twain's "bleak despair" are balanced by others like Bradford Smith, who view "The Stranger" as the final statement of a writer who knew "that the dark dungeon [of reality] undergirded the palace of pleasure [make-believe]." What, Smith asks, "but a surpassing sense of humor could blend these opposites into one . . . ?"

It is not surprising that there should be such a variety of views on "The Stranger." What is peculiar is that few critics attempt to deal directly with the problem of point of view in the tale. Bradford Smith seems simply to assume that Satan is Twain, and that Twain speaks through Satan; and Henry Nash Smith also seems to equate Satan with Twain. Such an equation is common in criticism on "The Stranger." That Satan is Twain's creation and not a personification of himself is rarely noted, even by critics of Henry Nash Smith's reputation; and Theodor, who narrates the bulk of the tale, is all but ignored by most commentators. Furthermore any attempt to analyze point of view in the story must depend heavily on a close examination of the work itself. Such an examination poses a few problems not encountered in most of Twain's other stories.

Unlike "The Stranger," the majority of the stories and sketches are not half-buried in the Mark Twain Papers at the University of California at Berkeley. Twain wrote several versions of the tale during his later years. None of these was complete and no version was published by Twain himself. In an attempt to solve some of the research difficulties caused by the existence of at least three unpublished versions of "The Stranger," John Tuckey, in *Mark Twain's "The Mysterious Stranger" and the Critics,* has constructed a composite of all of the various versions of the tale. As Tuckey explains: "For the text of 'The Mysterious Stranger' I have followed the 1916 edition of Paine and Duneka. I have, however . . . annotated the text to give some indication of the ways in which the 1916 edition differs from the manuscripts upon which it was based."

Although Tuckey takes much of the guesswork out of any structural analysis of the story, he states himself that an annotated text does not solve completely the textual problems of "The Stranger." Tuckey's text is primarily useful in that it is, despite whatever textual problems it does not solve, the most accurate text to date. However, its usefulness in studying point of view is limited. The presence and effectiveness of Twain's narrative voices is apparent in both the Paine-Duneka and the Tuckey-Paine-Duneka versions of "The Stranger." Theodor and Satan dominate the work to such an extent that their personalities are barely affected by Tuckey's annotations. It is ultimately the function of Theodor and Satan within the tale itself which must reveal their respective points of view.

Technically, there is only one central narrator of "The Stranger"; but there are two points of view within the story. Theodor Fischer tells the tale. However, it is Satan who provides Theodor with a new vision of his world. As Parsons observes, "Satan enters the dreaming boys' world of Eseldorf . . . and enlightens . . . Theodor Fischer, cruelly searing away every illusion." Together, Theodor and Satan are excellent examples of Twain's combined use of the innocent and experienced point of view. Perhaps this use of ostensibly opposite points of view is related to what Parsons calls Twain's need to illustrate both a hopeful and a hopeless solution for the problems of the damned human race.

In the naive Theodor, Twain has created a narrator who can record his childhood experiences from the vantage point of one who has great compassion for his fellow creatures. Theodor matures as he learns to view his world through Satan's eyes, but Theodor never abandons his compassionate point of view. Satan, on the other hand, is never naive. He possesses all knowledge, and he wishes to impart some of that knowledge to Theodor. Thus Theodor and Satan function almost as dramatic foils. Satan reveals Theodor to himself; but if Satan is nothing more than an illusion (or if he is what those of a psychological turn of mind might call Theodor's "alter ego"), it is Theodor who finally emerges, alone among the "empty eternities," as the most important, and perhaps even the most intriguing of Twain's two voices.

The use of two voices to present opposite points of view which eventually merge into one is not a technique which Twain developed solely in his late period. Gladys Bellamy points out that Twain's best work, early and late, was created by a simultaneous involvement with and detachment from his subject matter. Twain managed to cope with this paradoxical involved-detachment by a combination of techniques, most of which are apparent in "The Stranger." In works as far removed in time as *Huck Finn* and "The Stranger," Twain tells his story through some relatively simple character, such as Huck and Theodor. These simple characters can report actions or quote speeches of other characters—

characters so unlike themselves that the narrators do not understand what they reveal. To balance Theodor's view, Twain, in "The Stranger," has Satan view the human race with a complete and almost profound detachment. To further secure his own artistic detachment, Twain removes Eseldorf from his own time and place; and he reduces life to the unreality of a dream.

Satan's own existence is finally reduced to a dream; and it is Satan who must convince Theodor of that fact, for Theodor does not know until the end that he is dreaming at all. Satan is Theodor's guide through mysterious regions of the outer world of sense experience and the inner world of the mind. Satan is the devil-priest who, by the end of the story, baptizes Theodor into the "religion" of paradox. Like Prospero, Theodor becomes convinced that reality is "only a vision, a dream" and, as Satan tells the boy, "I myself have no existence; I am but a dream—your dream, creature of your imagination" (p. 678). With this final revelation, Theodor realizes that he and Satan are not really separable—they have merged into one being. Satan may be Theodor's creation; and to understand how Satan comes into being, either as a distinct individual or as a creature of Theodor's imagination it is essential to concentrate primarily, not on Satan (as do most critics), but on Theodor and his surroundings. It is, after all Theodor and his world that allow Satan to exist; and the "dream marks" are present from the beginning.

Chapter one of the tale begins with what seems an almost "stock opening" for Twain. Eseldorf, like so many of Twain's Mississippi River towns, is in the "middle of . . . sleep, being in the middle of Austria" (p. 602). The town "drowsed in peace in the deep privacy of a hilly and woodsy solitude where news of the world hardly ever came to disturb its dreams. . ." (p. 602). This dream-like setting is described by Theodor from memory, for he is, by his own account, "only a boy" when the events he speaks of take place. As in *Life on the Mississippi,* Twain uses a reflecting voice as narrator. Theodor, like the old river pilot of the earlier work, meditates on his youth. Despite this approach, the young Theodor of Eseldorf is the persona that emerges, for the man remembering his past sees that past through the eyes of a child—a child being initiated into the ways of a larger world of mind and matter. Theodor, after his experiences with Satan, seems to become an idealist with no illusions—a wise innocent. Vitelli, however, sees Theodor as a "Fool," and not a very wise one.

In "The Innocence of Mark Twain," Vitelli argues that Twain, in his "notoriously pessimistic" later work, "creates an image of the innocent as Fool, all the more foolish because he, the narrator, assumes a mask of wisdom." Vitelli seems only partially correct. In terms of the medieval concept of the "natural Fool" or "innocent," Twain follows an old tradition in creating such innocents as Theodor; but at no time do these innocent narrators assume "a mask of wisdom." Huck believes himself damned when he refuses to return Jim to his owner. The wise decision, measured by what is prudent, would be to betray his friend. Huck follows the dictates of his heart, not his intellect, wherein, presumably, wisdom is lodged. Similarly, Theodor's dominant trait is his compassion, hardly a "wise" characteristic if measured by the standards of the world Satan reveals to the boy. Perhaps if there can be such a thing as a "wise fool" both Huck and Theodor would qualify for the title; but their wisdom, if they possess any, springs from innocence, not false assumption. There is no image of the buffoon or of the wily frontiersman surrounding Theodor. Perhaps Vitelli reads too much of Twain himself into his fictional character. Because Twain once called himself (no doubt with his tongue planted firmly in his cheek) "a great and sublime fool" does not imply that he is attempting to make Theodor into his own image. Theodor, if he resembles anyone, resembles Huck Finn more than Mark Twain. Theodor is about Huck's age during the course of the tale; and, like Huck, Theodor is "not overmuch pestered with schooling" (p. 603). His language, although he is supposed to be Austrian born, often sounds much like Huck's dialect. Words such as "pestered" sometime find their way into Theodor's vocabulary; and like the Mississippi River truant he resembles, Theodor and his friends often stretch out "on the grass in the shade to rest and smoke and talk over . . . strange things. . ." (p. 606). Theodor's dreamlike world of boyish adventure undergoes no change until the arrival of Satan.

Early, and repeatedly, Twain emphasizes the undisturbed atmosphere of fantasy permeating the whole of Eseldorf:

The whole region . . . was the hereditary property of a prince, whose servants kept the castle always in perfect condition for occupancy, but neither he nor his family came there oftener than once in five years. When they came it was as if the lord of the world had arrived, and had brought all the glories of its kingdoms along; and when they went they left a calm behind which was like the deep sleep which follows an orgy (pp. 602-603).

Eseldorf, Theodor says, "was paradise for us boys"; and the paradise seems populated by a set of characters that could easily have sprung, as Satan points out at the end of the tale, from Theodor's imagination. There is Father Adolf, whom Tuckey says Twain made the villain of the story in the original manuscripts. Invented by Paine and Duneka is the astrologer, "who does not appear in the tale as Twain wrote it." Paine and Duneka transfer the evil attached to Father Adolf to the astrologer, presumably because they felt that such a character would be less offensive than an evil priest. To contrast with Father Adolf is Father Peter, a gentle priest whose enemy is the astrologer. In at least one version of the story, if Tuckey is accurate, Father Adolf and not the astrologer is Father Peter's enemy. Finally, to round off such a group of characters (among whom are many not mentioned above) is Satan himself, nephew to the fallen angel, and eventually mentor to the young Theodor. Truly, as Satan observes at the close of the story, the setting and cast of characters in this strange tale could well be creatures of Theodor's imagination—citizens of his dreams.

Satan's appearance into this fantastic world of Eseldorf is made, not with great fanfare, but quietly. He appears, significantly, not to teach the elders and priests of the village, but to instruct a group of children who have not yet been completely "corrupted" by the "Moral Sense." They are children who are not bound by the rules of behavior developed by a selfish society. Their concepts of good and evil have not become solidified to conform to the world around them. They make no moral judgments based on traditional moral concepts. Their innocence is almost sublime. It is their innocence which allows them to learn from Satan.

To reinforce the idea that Satan may well be a part of the boys' collective imagination, Twain stresses that the angel cannot be seen by anyone unless he desires to be seen; or perhaps, if Satan is a creature of the imagination, it is the desire of others to see him which accounts for his visibility. In any case, Satan restricts his early appearances to Theodor and his close friends; and even after Satan appears to the townspeople as Philip Traum, the boys cannot reveal his true identity to anyone outside of their own circle. Early in the tale, Father Peter "walked straight through Satan," and, as Theodor explains:

It made us catch our breath to see it. We had the impulse to cry out, the way you nearly always do when a startling thing happens, but something mysterious restrained us and we remained quiet, only breathing fast. Then the trees hid Father Peter after a little, and Satan said:
"It is as I told you—I am only a spirit . . . none of us was visible to him, for I wished it so" (p. 614).

Just as Satan "wished" to remain invisible to Father Peter so also does he wish the boys to remain silent about what he teaches them. Again, as Theodor explains:

We had seen wonders this day; and my thoughts began to run on the pleasure it would be to tell them when I got home, but he [Satan] noticed those thoughts, and said:

"No, all these matters are secret among us four. I do not mind your trying to tell them, if you like, but I will protect your tongues, and nothing of the secret will escape from them" (p. 613).

Satan's function is almost solely restricted to the art of teaching. He is a teacher whose "audio-visual aids" are created out of earth and air. To demonstrate the objectivity and detachment of such an instructor, Twain has Satan create a small community of miniature humans, only to destroy them all by earthquake. When the boys protest that the poor creatures have died and gone to hell, Satan responds that "they were of no value . . . we can make plenty more" (p. 612). The tears of the horror-struck boys do not move Satan for "It was of no use to try to move him; evidently he was wholly without feeling, and could not understand. He was full of bubbling spirits, and as gay as if this were a wedding instead of a fiendish massacre" (p. 612). The angel's is the perfectly detached voice of one who is not concerned with human activity, but only amused by it. Satan compares man to a wood-louse; and he expands upon the difference between man and himself by emphasizing the chasm which separates the human from the divine:

Man is made of dirt—I saw him made. I am not made of dirt. Man is a museum of diseases, a home of impurities; he comes to-day and is gone to-morrow; he begins as dirt and departs as stench; I am of the aristocracy of the imperishables. And man has the Moral Sense. You understand? He has the Moral Sense. That would seem to be difference enough between us, all by itself (p. 615).

Satan has an advantage few of Twain's voices have. He can speak of man from the vantage point of an immortal who is not obliged to conform to human logic or to human "Moral Sense." Satan (whose "public" name, Traum, means Dream) is capable of doing anything he pleases; and he can criticize the human race by making such a sweeping statement as "to kill [is] the chiefest ambition of the human race and the earliest incident in its history—but only the Christian civilization has scored a triumph to be proud of. Two or three centuries from now it will be recognized that all the competent killers are Christians . . ." (p. 663). When Satan speaks in such a tone, he sounds very much like his creator, who once called America (a Christian nation) "The United States of Lyncherdom"; and Satan is freer to express such attitudes than any conventional narrator. To say, however, that Satan merely serves as a device through which Twain can vent his anger at the world at large would be to ignore the other half of Twain's narrative voice—Theodor. Certainly Satan's idea regarding man's low position on the evolutionary scale is Twain's own belief. His essays and newspaper articles prove that point; but Theodor's unfailing compassion which Satan ironically helps to strengthen cannot be ignored, even in the light of Satan's almost overpowering and unfeeling objectivity. Satan is insensitive to suffering, but he sensitizes Theodor to suffering by transporting the boy about torture chambers and French factories, where Christian culture has been perverted, and where cruelty claims falsely to be Christian. When Satan says, "It is the Moral Sense which teaches the factory proprietors the difference between right and wrong—you perceive the result" (p. 629), he is being sarcastic, utilizing the term "Moral Sense" ironically. He means rational, prudent, enlightened self-interest. Satan enjoys toying with the ambiguities of terms like "conscience" and "Moral Sense." He uses them to refer to the socially implanted codes of dealing with others that pretend to be selfless but are selfish. Theodor is, largely and ironically because Satan exposes him to his own race, compassionate to what Satan calls the human race's "conscience-soothing falsities, and . . . grotesque self-deception" (p. 668).

Although Henry Nash Smith and others seem to insist that Twain is identifying with the unfeeling supernatural observer, it is Theodor who is central to the story; and perhaps the boy's importance indicates that Twain is still protesting suffering and cruelty, despite the rationally foolish and absurd demands of the Christian ethic. Technically, the central consciousness is Theodor's, and it is a feeling consciousness. When Satan laughs at the human race, Theodor is quick to observe that "No one but an angel could have acted so; but suffering is nothing to them; they do not know what it is, except by hearsay" (p. 662). Satan cannot feel empathy for creatures so far beneath him, and Theodor cannot help being empathetic. It is possible, if these two are considered as contrasting halves of a dualistic narrative voice, that together they give form to Twain's paradoxical concept of his world; and "The Mysterious Stranger" may well serve to illustrate, not the "notorious pessimism" of an old and failing writer, but the culmination of an artistic approach which had its origins in the very early works. What Satan teaches Theodor about man's "Moral Sense" Huck learned from the "King" and the "Duke." "A person's conscience," Huck says, "ain't got no sense;" and what seems to many to be the rantings of an old and angry man, venting his spleen in "The Mysterious Stranger," is merely the culmination of an artistic vision formulated in part on the Mississippi River and Nevada frontier long before Twain began to write. It is a vision stripped of self delusion and conceit.

SELECTED BIBLIOGRAPHY

1. GENERAL STUDIES

Blair, Walter, ed. Introduction. *Selected Shorter Writings of Mark Twain.* New York: Houghton Mifflin, 1962, pp. vii-xxvi.

Fenger, Gerald J. *The Perspectives of Satire in Mark Twain's Short Stories.* Dissertation. Texas Christian University, 1974.

Neider, Charles, ed. Introduction. *The Complete Short Stories of Mark Twain.* New York: Bantam, 1971, pp. xi-xxii.

Reiss, Edmund, ed. Foreward. *The Mysterious Stranger and Other Stories.* New York: Signet, 1962, pp. vii-xv.

2. "THE CELEBRATED JUMPING FROG"

Baender, Paul. "The 'Jumping Frog' as a Comedian's First Virtue," *Modern Philology,* 60 (Feb. 1963), 192-200.

Blair, Walter. *Native American Humor.* New York: American Book Company, 1937, pp. 156-57.

Branch, Edgar M. *The Literary Aprenticeship of Mark Twain.* Urbana, IL: University of Illinois Press, 1950, pp. 120-27.

———. "'My Voice is Still for Setchell': A Background Study of 'Jim Smiley and His Jumping Frog.'" *PMLA,* 82 (Dec. 1967), 591-601.

Clemens, S. L. "Private History of the 'Jumping Frog' Story." *Literary Essays.* Author's National Edition. Vol. 24. New York: Harper, 1897, 100-110.

Cohen, Hennig. "Twain's Jumping Frog: Folktale to Life to Folktale." *Western Folklore,* 22 (Jan. 1963), 17-18.

Cuff, Roger Penn. "Mark Twain's Use of California Folklore in His Jumping Frog Story." *Journal of American Folklore,* 65 (1952), 155-58.

Covici, Pascal. *Mark Twain's Humor: The Image of a World.* Dallas: Southern Methodist University Press, 1962, pp. 48-52.

DeVoto, Bernard. *Mark Twain's America.* Boston: Little, Brown, 1932, pp. 174-78.

Gibson, William. *The Art of Mark Twain.* New York: Oxford University Press, 1976, 73-75.

Lewis, Oscar. *The Origin of the Celebrated Jumping Frog.* San Francisco: The Book Club of California, 1931.

Rourke, Constance. *American Humor: A Study of the National Character.* New York: Harcourt Brace, 1931, pp. 204-21.

Schmidt, Paul. "The Deadpan on Simon Wheeler." *Southwest Review,* 41 (Summer 1956), 270-77.

3. "A TRUE STORY"

Bellamy, Gladys. *Mark Twain as a Literary Artist.* Norman OK: University of Oklahoma Press, 1950, pp. 299-300.

Budd, Louis. *Mark Twain: Social Philosopher.* Bloomington IN: Indiana University Press, 1962, p. 92.

Paine, Albert Bigelow. *Mark Twain: A Biography.* New York: Harper, 1912, I, 513-14.

Rogers, Franklin. *Mark Twain's Burlesque Patterns.* Dallas: Southern Methodist University Press, 1960, p. 92.

4. "FACTS CONCERNING THE RECENT CARNIVAL OF CRIME"

Baetzhold, Howard. *Mark Twain and John Bull.* Bloomington IN: Indiana University Press, 1970, p. 58.

Blair, Walter, ed. Introduction. *Selected Shorter Writings of Mark Twain.* New York: Houghton Mifflin, 1962, p. xxi.

Blues, Thomas. *Mark Twain and the Community.* Lexington KY: University Press of Kentucky, pp. 22-23.

Covici, Pascal. *Mark Twain's Humor: The Image of a World.* Dallas: Southern Methodist University Press, 1962, pp. 236-37.

Kaplan, Justin. *Mr. Clemens and Mark Twain.* New York: Simon & Schuster, 1966, p. 196.

Paine, Albert Bigelow. *Mark Twain: A Biography.* New York: Harper, 1912, II, 732-33.

5. "THE £1,000,000 BANK-NOTE"

Covici, Pascal. *Mark Twain's Humor: The Image of a World.* Dallas: Southern Methodist University Press, 1962, p. 207.

Reiss, Edmund, ed. Foreward. *The Mysterious Stranger and Other Stories.* New York: Signet, 1962, p. vii.

6. "THE MAN THAT CORRUPTED HADLEYBURG"

Bertolotti, D. S. "Structural Unity in 'The Man That Corrupted Hadleyburg.' " *Mark Twain Journal,* 14 (Winter 1967-68), 19-21.

Clark, George Pierce. "The Devil That Corrupted Hadleyburg." *Mark Twain Journal,* 10 (Winter 1956-57), 1-4.

Covici, Pascal. *Mark Twain's Humor: The Image of a World.* Dallas: Southern Methodist University Press, 1962, pp. 189-205.

Foner, Philip. *Mark Twain: Social Critic.* International Publishers, 1958, pp. 140-42.

Gibson, William. *The Art of Mark Twain.* New York: Oxford University Press, 1977, pp. 90-95.

Macnaughton, William R. *Mark Twain's Last Years As a Writer.* Columbia MO: University of Missouri Press, 1979, pp. 100-103.

Park, Martha M. "Mark Twain's Hadleyburg: A House Built on Sand." *CLA Journal,* 16 (June 1973), 508-13.

Parsons, Coleman O. "The Devil and Samuel Clemens." *Virginia Quarterly Review,* 23 (Autumn 1947), 595-600.

Rucker, Mary E. "Moralism and Determinism in 'The Man That Corrupted Hadleyburg.'" *Studies in Short Fiction,* 14 (Winter 1977), 49-54.

Varisco, Raymond. "A Militant Voice: Mark Twain's 'The Man That Corrupted Hadleyburg.'" *Revista/Review Interamericana,* 8 (1978), 129-37.

Wecter, Dixon. *Sam Clemens of Hannibal.* Boston: Houghton Mifflin, 1952, 222-23.

Werge, Thomas. "The Sin of Hypocrisy in 'The Man That Corrupted Hadleyburg' and *Inferno XXIII.*'" *Mark Twain Journal,* 18 (Winter 1975-76), 17-18.

7. "THE $30,000 BEQUEST"

Covici, Pascal. *Mark Twain's Humor: The Image of a World.* Dallas: Southern Methodist University Press, 1962, pp. 24-25.

Foner, Philip. *Mark Twain: Social Critic.* New York: International Publishers, 1958, pp. 160-61.

Macnaughton, William R. *Mark Twain's Last Years As a Writer.* Columbia MO: University of Missouri Press, 1979, pp. 197-98.

8. "EXTRACTS FROM CAPTAIN STORMFIELD'S VISIT TO HEAVEN"

Baldanza, Frank. *Mark Twain: An Introduction and Interpretation.* New York: Barnes & Noble, 1961, pp. 128-31.

Geismar, Maxwell. *Mark Twain: American Prophet.* Boston: Houghton Mifflin, 1970, pp. 284-88.

Wecter, Dixon. Introduction. *Report from Paradise.* New York: Harper, 1952.

9. "THE MYSTERIOUS STRANGER"

Note: For studies preceding 1967, see John S. Tuckey, *Mark Twain's "The Mysterious Stranger" and the Critics.* Belmont CA: Wadsworth, 1968.

Geismar, Maxwell. *Mark Twain: American Prophet.* Boston: Houghton Mifflin, 1970, pp. 331-56.

Gervais, Ronald J. "*The Mysterious Stranger:* The Fall into Salvation." *Pacific Coast Philology,* 5 (1970), 24-33.

Gibson, William M. *The Art of Mark Twain.* New York: Oxford University Press, 1976, pp. 186-201.

Livingston, James L. "Names in Mark Twain's 'The Mysterious Stranger,'" *American Notes and Queries,* 12 (March 1974), 108-109.

Nebeker, Helen E. "The Great Corrupter or Satan Rehabilitated." *Studies in Short Fiction,* 8 (1971), 635-37.

Perkins, Vivienne. "The Trouble with Satan: Structural and Semantic Problems in *The Mysterious Stranger.*" *Gypsy Scholar,* 3 (1975), 37-43.

Rowlette, Robert. "Mark Twain's Barren Tree in *The Mysterious Stranger:* Two Biblical Parallels." *Mark Twain Journal,* 16 (Winter 1971-72), 19-20.

Scott, Arthur L. *Mark Twain at Large.* Chicago: Henry Regnery Company, 1969, 243-45.

Scrivener, Buford. "'The Mysterious Stranger': Mark Twain's New Myth of the Fall." *Mark Twain Journal,* 17 (Fall 1975), 20-21.

Tuckey, John S. "Hannibal, Weggis, and Mark Twain's Eseldorf." *American Literature,* 42 (1970), 235-40.

Wilson, James D. "Hank Morgan, Philip Traum and Milton's Satan." *Mark Twain Journal,* 16 (Summer 1973), 20-21.

INDEX